Managing Communication

IN LOCAL GOVERNMENT

LOCAL GOVERNMENT MANAGEMENT SERIES

This series provides local government managers with the help required to understand the rapidly changing context in which they work. The current pressures on managers, created by the changing public expectation of services and the policy and budgetary framework, require a major expansion of their responsibilities and make more demands on their know-how and skills. The books will guide these managers through the processes of the practical handling of increasingly complex management tasks and issues. Valuable insights into successful management practice and a sound understanding of the local government context are combined to enable first-level managers and above to fulfil their new roles effectively and efficiently.

SERIES EDITORS

The series editors have both been senior managers in local government. **Paul Corrigan** has worked in economic development at the GLC, been Deputy Director of ILEAS's education social work services and was Head of Quality Management at the London Borough of Islington. He was lead consultant in the establishment of the Camden Education Department. In recent years he has worked as a management consultant in local government. **Paul Joyce** was employed as Chief Training Officer and Assistant Director of Personnel at the London Borough of Islington in the early 1990s. He is now Director of the Management Research Centre at the University of North London. Both editors have been involved in research on the management of local government, both being interested in applied research which is of use to those with responsibility for the success and effectiveness of local government.

LOCAL GOVERNMENT MANAGEMENT SERIES

Managing Communication

IN LOCAL GOVERNMENT

MARK FLETCHER

PUBLISHED IN ASSOCIATION WITH THE IDA IMPROVEMENT AND DEVELOPMENT AGENCY

KOGAN
PAGE

This book is dedicated to the memory of Phil Rice

YOURS TO HAVE TO HOLD

BUT NOT TO COPY

First published in 1999

Kogan Page Limited
120 Pentonville Road
London N1 9JN

© Mark Fletcher, 1999

British Library Cataloguing in Publication Data

A CIP record for this book is available from the British Library.

ISBN 0 7494 2914 3

Typeset by Kogan Page
Printed and bound by Biddles Ltd, Guildford and King's Lynn

Contents

Series editors' foreword

At the turn of the new millennium, all organizations that serve the public will be under very great stress. The public expect them to provide high-quality services, whether they are banks or supermarkets, schools or residential homes. The service industry in the private sector sets standards of customer service which have to be met by public sector organizations, and if they fail, the public quickly lets them know. It is no longer possible for public service managers to expect the public to be simply grateful for any service they deliver. As a consequence services are being organized with a great deal more public involvement and consultation than in the past.

Local government is no exception. People not only expect their streets to be kept efficiently clean, but they expect them to be cleaned with courtesy; they not only expect social housing to be warm and well-repaired, but expect tenants to be treated with the same service expectations as owner-occupiers. They also expect local government to involve them as citizens and provide community leadership in dealing with a wide range of issues including crime and the environment that stretch beyond the orthodox services that they deliver.

These are long-term changes and call for very different local government organizational structures. These structures need to move away from the old hierarchical closed form to one that involves the public and staff in a wide variety of different task-centred groups. Indeed, without public involvement it is difficult to see how most local government services can be delivered – without parental involvement, education standards will not rise as high; without tenant involvement, estates become areas of high crime; without carers in the real community, our elderly and vulnerable cannot be looked after.

All of this calls for very different forms of public management in local government – both in terms of style and skill. These changes need to be carried out not just by the managers at the top of the organization, but throughout its entire structure. Middle managers need to develop a wide range of very different approaches to their organization and its services.

Managers in local government, therefore, not only find themselves in the midst of great pressures for change, but also engaged in efforts to promote the more modern public services while developing their own role and skills. We must not lose sight of the fact that while the political and legal tide is running strongly in the direction of modernization, the meaning of this modernization is often fluid. The changes which are occurring are full of tensions and sometimes contradictory conditions. At one moment the emphasis is on improvements in service delivery, at another it is dealing with failures of services below required standards of public services, and yet at other times it is about innovative ways of addressing community issues. Then again, we see modernization stressing the need for the use of competitive forces, and then the importance of partnership and coordination. This by no means exhausts the fluidity and complexity of conditions. Yet it makes it clear that there are critical decisions to be made by managers. In making decisions in the midst of all this change, we are of the opinion that managers in local government should act consciously with an understanding of the fact that they share in a responsibility for modernization, and that the public and politicians have expectations that managers will respond positively to the responsibility and not seek to perpetuate past patterns of activity.

These expectations of the manager are challenging ones. Possibly, the expectations of the public and politicians have never been more demanding. Years ago, managers generally (not just in the public sector) conceptualized their role in terms of command and control structures. The same overall technique was always considered applicable: plan, carry out, monitor and take corrective action. This was the template for management as applied to matters such as budgets, production, quality and stock levels. Within this overall model of management, the job of supervision within local government, as elsewhere, was seen as keeping the services flowing by solving problems and correcting deviations. The emphasis was, therefore, on controlling people, processes and resources.

In more recent times, when people looked critically at management in the private and public sectors, confidence in the detail and specifics of management practices was undermined. Attempts were then made through the Management Charter Initiative to set standards of management practice in great detail. Vocational competencies were itemized for managers, spelling out a new customary standard for management throughout the UK. The measure of the truth of these competencies was sought through an appeal to representatives of the management community as a whole to validate these written specifications of management practice. This appeal for validation aimed to produce a recognition which could form the social authority for the standards.

The expectations, which now have force, seem to have moved or be moving beyond this 'stage' of management as a set of customary or conventional practices. This is because these expectations are first and foremost concerned with making public services more modern, and by placing the development of management within the modernization agenda the issue of management responsibility comes to the fore. As critical agents of modernization, local government managers are expected to make logical and accountable decisions, to develop appropriate organizational and service cultures, to use their power within and on behalf of local government structures with care, and to develop individual employees and organizations (innovation). Thus the accent is on the responsibilities of the manager as much as it is on their role in control and in the performance of the details of management. This new management requires many new different skills if these responsibilities are to be discharged.

This series addresses the needs for these different skills. Each book will achieve three interlinked aims:

1. It will demonstrate the different context for new local government that is developing at the turn of the new millennium.
2. It will show how local government needs to organize itself differently to work within this context.
3. Above all, it will communicate the new skills that middle level local government managers need to work within these new organizations.

To achieve this, each book will develop its arguments not simply through the text but with case studies or tasks which managers will be expected to work through to ensure that they have come to grips with the ideas in the text.

The books have been written by practitioners and will, therefore, be practical, providing managers with real examples of practice and developing ways in which they can develop these new ways of working.

Paul Corrigan and Paul Joyce
January 1999

Preface

COMMUNICATION IN THE REAL WORLD

Whatever your plans, ambitions, talent or resources success will elude you if your communication is poor. The wrong word in the wrong place, poor timing, or even just talking too loud or too often can cause others to think that you are insensitive, ham-fisted or inept and whatever you were planning to do can go to the wall.

This book is about trying to help managers overcome some of the difficulties surrounding communication by asking readers to think of it in a new way. I will be asking readers to go beyond a simple definition of communication as the transmission of information. Instead, this is about getting people to think of communication as one way of getting things to happen. In other words, communication is purposeful and pragmatic. It is a means to an end. I am not suggesting that we should run our lives around that notion but it seems to me that approaching situations as opportunities and using communication as a tool can offer professionals a new way of considering how they get their message across.

The book is rooted in the real world. It would be nice if we lived in a blame-free culture, if the people who worked for us went out and sold the virtues of our organization to their friends and neighbours, and if our world was not populated by hidden agendas. However, none of these is the case. Blame is alive and well and living in virtually every workplace in the country. Yes, we should change it but it will not change next week. It will take a lot longer and in the meantime we still have to get things done and we still have to communicate.

We would all wish that our employees thought that our council was the best thing since sliced bread. Given the number of people who work in local government, if every employee said one nice thing about their council each week our public image would be off the scale within a month but sadly that is not going to happen. This book is not embedded in a 'motherhood and apple pie' view of life. The techniques and ideas you will read are designed to engage with the cynicism that you will encounter every day before lunch.

Finally, politics (with a small 'p') is everywhere. In every meeting you will take part in you will meet other agendas. In any situation where advancement depends upon difference there will be those who will malign your work. No doubt you will do so of others. Your reputation will be under constant assault. You will need to protect it if you are to thrive, or even survive. There is little point in pretending that others will see your work and recognize its excellence in an unquestioned way. You will need to take them to it and show them what you have achieved and you will have to do so quickly and in a planned way. Others will be there before you talking about its shortcomings. Damning by faint praise is as much a part of the culture as committee meetings.

This book is a collection of tools. You may choose to use none of them. But you should at least know that they are there. Others will, in any event, be already hard at work, preening their reputation and creating the climate within which they want to work. Communication is at the heart of all that building but like all skills it needs to be learned, practised and refined.

Chapter 1 begins by looking at the idea of how we manage our credibility. Like reputation our credibility in the corridors of power counts for a lot. I will suggest that we live in a credibility marketplace where, like traders, we will attempt to increase the value of our stock. When we deliver our promises our stock goes up. When we fail it drops and when others, who may have high credibility, say they don't rate us, our stock will fall still further. This chapter examines how this works and what you can do about it when your market value starts to plummet.

Chapter 2 takes a departure from traditional thinking on PR. If we believe we live, whether we like it or not, in a blame-culture we should think about how others see us. It would be nice if we didn't have to but then it would be nice if the sun always shone. Idealism is fine but it doesn't count for much in the cut and thrust of management in action. This chapter focuses on how you manage your own reputation and how it can come under threat from many sides.

Chapters 3 and 4 look at internal communication and the need to win the battle for the hearts and minds of local government staff. The most effective managers will recognize that local people's perceptions are shaped at the *point of contact* with front-line staff. However, in a world where resources are being sliced away and posts are under threat, how to create a climate where those staff will want to represent the authority positively is a key question. Some of the tools and techniques which may be used are looked at closely.

Chapters 5 and 6 look at media relations, to many a bugbear, to others an opportunity but to all a challenge. Media relations are inevitable. As long as local government reaches into every part of daily life then it will be of interest to the media. Try to pretend otherwise and you will confirm that you are in the wrong job. These chapters look at ways of understanding and using those relationships.

Chapter 7 puts communication strategies into a *real world* context. While a communication strategy will help you to get your message across to a specific audience if it is to be effective the strategy has to take account of the different elements of pollution which may prevent your message reaching your audience. 'Mind the gaps' is an attempt to provide managers with a framework within which communication can be planned.

Chapter 8 examines some of the challenges facing local government in the years ahead. In one sense we can all shape our future. And, if all members of staff were committed to that mission, local government could vastly increase its value with local people. One thing is clear. There are more opportunities every day for individual members of staff to affect perceptions of their authority than those presented by the media. The last chapter looks at four key themes – working with a modern workforce to communicate the message; creating and maintaining the local authority; engaging the local community; and the importance of locality for local media and local authorities.

Chapter 9 looks at how we make sense of communication by examining definitions of PR and how rethinking it can make it a more useful concept for all managers. This chapter is not naïve. It doesn't suggest that if everyone talks to each other then life will be good. Rather, it tries to locate communication in the real world and in that world resources are stretched, promises are made and broken and politics (with a small and large 'p') is ever present. At the end of this chapter I look at how we make sense of communication through common sense.

In the final analysis this book is not rocket science. It is a collection of ideas and techniques. There is nothing in here which the best local government managers don't do every single day. All *Managing Communication* does is to allow readers to examine their own practices and look for ways of learning new skills and outlooks.

Acknowledgements

Writing books is a lot harder than I thought and there is no doubt that without the support of Paul Corrigan I would never have got started, let alone have finished this project. So my hat will remain off to Paul for a long time. I would also like to thank Paul Joyce of the University of North London for interesting and thought-provoking comments.

Many of the ideas in this book have been floating around my head for a long time and I have bounced them off various people during the last few years. In doing so I have amended and gradually refined them. Many have helped me in this process. I would like to acknowledge the contribution of the late Phil Rice with whom I taught a communication management programme at Coventry University. I would also like to thank Lorraine Langham and Marina Pirotta and Fran Collingham for their patient listening and helpful suggestions. I am also grateful to Carol Grant, Mike McCabe, Michael Baker, Pete Mitchell, and Robert Underwood for their case studies, and to Phil Ellis for his helpful comments. I'd like to thank Kogan Page for publishing the book. Finally, I'd like to thank my wife Hilary and our four children Rachael, Roberta, Gregor and Ailis who put up with a distracted person about the house during the writing and revision of this book.

1 Trading in the credibility marketplace

What people say about you matters. You might be doing the best job in the world but if everybody is talking you down, and saying that you're not, then you may as well not bother. This chapter begins from the point that what we do and what others say about us will, on a daily basis, shape our reputation. It examines the idea that each of us trades in the credibility marketplace. As we deliver our promises our credibility goes up. With every unfulfilled promise it goes down.

In examining the concept of credibility management and trading the chapter focuses on a number of different elements. The first part of this chapter focuses on why credibility matters. Secondly, I will look at the ways we understand credibility. If we are to understand why we make the judgements we do, we need to focus on our own practices and so there are two exercises which allow readers to examine the basis upon which we award credibility to others. The chapter then looks at ways in which credibility is both gained and lost. This leads to an examination of the way in which credibility can be developed in a marketplace. The chapter then moves on to examine ways in which we might accumulate credibility by looking at four main themes – knowledge, wisdom, ways of behaving and the importance of symbols (which includes a brief history of the Local Government Association's corporate identity). Finally, in this chapter, I examine how we trade in the credibility marketplace – how we gain and lose credibility in the eyes of others. In particular, I will look at how we might develop strategies to help us acquire credibility with different audiences.

WHY HAVING CREDIBILITY MATTERS

A good deal of this book is concerned with the ways in which information is both presented and put in context. As far as both first impressions and tangen-

tial relationships are concerned, the chapter points out the tactics and techniques it is possible to use to present a particular face of reality. However, in
the longer term, and indeed in terms of ongoing personal relationships, there
is no merit in simply concentrating on the simple presentation of reality. The
crucial message for all managers of communication is that it is the substance
and integrity of our realities which will cause people to feel the things they feel
about us.

Critically, senior managers who simply concentrate on the messages they
send out to their staff without taking account of how their staff might receive
and interpret those messages will run into difficulties. Worse, if managers fail
to listen to the signals coming back from staff then that's when the real problems will start. The same is true of the public. If the PR message from the
council is that all services are of high quality, but the experience that the public
have of council services is patchy, then the public will learn their message from
their own experience and not from the message of the council. Once the public have found that the council are trying to sell them a false message on this issue, the result will be their rejection of all other messages from the council.

In the end, we are not so much managing communication as we are managing the confidence that others will invest in us. Others will not invest in us unless they believe us to be credible and truthful and, inevitably, any practice
which is concerned with the presentation of reality will draw suspicion from
those to whom realities are presented. At the very least people will compare
the reality you are presenting to them with the reality that they experience.
That is why it is critical that alongside any plans to present a particular face
there should be the realization that our own credibility is a critical factor in the
success or failure to convince and communicate.

This chapter is concerned with that issue of credibility. I suggest that we not
only seek to present ourselves as credible but that we trade in credibility on a
day-to-day basis. This analysis clearly has to have a theoretical basis. I have
chosen the concept of the marketplace because we believe that as in all marketplaces we trade our currency in order to make purchases. Although we may
trade credibility to make purchases, in the context of local government, and
particularly in management, we gain agreement to do things. This makes the
analogy with currency to buy products a good one since credibility, like
money, on its own is not worth very much. It is what it buys that is important. It
is on the basis of our credibility that our peers, managers and the members of
the local authority will allow us to take action.

When a report comes before a committee presented by, say, the director of
education, that report will stand or fall not only on the basis of the recommendations standing before councillors, but also on whether they believe that the
individual has credibility with the various audiences touched by the report.
For example, a report calling on the education committee to allow the director of education to establish a county-wide heads' steering group will be con-

sidered in the context of whether councillors believe in a number of factors concerned with the director's credibility.

- Have they successfully set up something before and has it worked?
- What is their relationship with heads like?
- Will they be able to set up such a group but not try and run it from the centre?
- If the director does allow the heads to have their own forum, can he or she deal with the conflict that comes from it?

The committee will have previous experience of all these factors and will judge their response on its basis.

WAYS OF UNDERSTANDING CREDIBILITY

At its roots credibility is about belief. It is about the belief that others have in us to do something or to be something. If, for example, we make a promise to do something and then do it, others will be able to say, 'that person made that promise and delivered'. If we repeat this action over and over again we will be perceived to be reliable, that is others will be able to predict how we will behave on the basis of things we have said and done. That is different from being able to predict how we will behave simply on the basis of things we have said.

That is not to say that we won't believe unless we first see action. In other circumstances we are prepared to place our faith in the fact that promises will be delivered without first seeing action. For example, the election of a Labour government in 1997 came about because sufficient numbers of people felt able to trust the words of senior Labour politicians. If polls are to believed much of that trust was invested in one man, Tony Blair, and, where we continue to invest our trust in one person, the behaviour of that single individual will be a critical factor in our judgements about the credibility of the government as a whole.

We are able to place trust and, therefore, attribute credibility to individuals where they have not taken specific action related to their promises but where they have demonstrated action in other fields. If, for example, you ask one of your staff to undertake project work on a new area of business where they have no experience you would invest trust for other reasons such as:

- it may be that they have demonstrated the ability to work alone;
- it may be that they are able to work to deadlines;
- it may be that they are able to demonstrate sound and balanced judgement.

3

And because of these three factors you may well believe that they are capable of carrying out the work. You believe they have credibility. What you will be doing is benchmarking their credibility against other dissimilar activities. In other words, it doesn't matter whether the person you are judging in one field is doing the same as another person in a different field. We will compare performances in terms of promises followed by actions.

We will also invest in trust and believe others to be credible because of third-party endorsements. Where we believe one person to be credible we are likely to accept their word that another individual is credible. This, after all, is the basis upon which the reference system is built. It also suggests that if we are able to accumulate a number of independent and credible people who are prepared to say positive things about our performance, then our credibility will in turn go up.

Another factor in awarding credibility will be how many existing recognized symbols are attributed to a particular person. In the commercial world companies will try to build trust in their products via brands. When we see the Boots' brand we will associate it with cleanliness, science, pharmacy and so on. So if the managing director of Boots came to talk to our members about partnerships, for example, we are likely to imbue him or her with our perceptions of the company. They will, by default, be deemed to be credible.

In most local authorities some services (and some individuals) have much better reputations than others. On occasions a few services have a strong reputation and the council as a whole has a bad one. Under these circumstances it is not surprising that the services with high credibility may want to separate themselves from the council as a whole. This gives them the opportunity to develop their own credibility separate from the diminishing aspect of the council as a whole. It is likely that the council corporately will resist such a separation, since it would leave them as a whole with very little credibility, but it is nonetheless something which happens. Directors of leisure services will argue that it's important that their services are branded differently as they need to get 'bums on seats'. Leisure is a much more 'sexy' product. The danger for the authority is that if all the 'interesting bits' are branded differently then the rump that is left will inevitably seem 'boring', or worse, incompetent.

Credibility is something which exists as a result of a process or a series of judgements. Few of us will invest our trust and believe others to be credible where there are no assets which are recognizably credible. We will award credibility to others in the context of those things we already know to be credible. In one sense we benchmark others against ourselves and what we know or think can be done in a given set of circumstances.

The following exercise gives you the opportunity to examine your own credibility criteria.

Exercise – examining your own credibility criteria

Imagine you have received a letter, delivered by hand, asking you to arrange a meeting with the leader of your council on matters of mutual interest. Assume that he has accurately spelt your name, that the letter has today's date on it and that there is a phone number given. The letter is set out as follows:

Dear Mr Smith,

I am writing to you because I believe you will be able to help me and my company work more closely with your council.

There may, I believe, be matters of mutual benefit. I have taken the time to undertake a substantial piece of research on your anti-poverty strategy and, given the chance to explain my thinking to the leader of your council, believe I will be able to assist you in helping your community.

I look forward to hearing from you. You may write to me at the above address or phone me on my mobile number which is 0900 900900.

With best wishes,

Dr Michael Smith.

Write down (a) whether you believed the letter, (b) what factors make the letter credible and (c) what features may give you cause for concern.

This exercise will have told you something about the factors which are important to you in awarding credibility to the author. Are those factors important to your colleagues, or indeed, your council?

It is one thing to hold your own view about what is and is not credible. But in your everyday work you will have to make a number of judgements where you will expect others to share your point of view. Think about how you actually share that information. How much of it is written down in management guidance and how much is simply 'the way we do things here'?

CREDIBILITY GAIN AND LOSS

There is no question that just as we can gain credibility so, too, can we lose it. Tabloid papers exist on a diet of 'how the mighty have fallen' stories. As onlookers we are very interested in people who were once great and now have come back down to earth. Equally, we have seen individuals who, over a period of years, have started from humble beginnings and gone on to great things. There are others still, perhaps who come from particular classes, who will always be deemed credible. Royals and members of our upper class may well be in this category. However, even they, particularly in the aftermath of the death of the Princess of Wales, have shown how easy it is to fall from the grace of high credibility.

As a rule it is probably easier to lose credibility than it is to earn it. The process of accumulation may, for some, take many years. Every high-profile person who has made one silly remark to the wrong person at the wrong time will know that credibility free-fall is only one edition away.

THE CREDIBILITY MARKETPLACE

One way of looking at credibility is as a series of marketplaces. We are all players in marketplaces for credibility. We do not all trade in the same marketplace. At work we will trade in an office marketplace with its own conception of what is and is not credible. Some of the behaviours deemed to be highly credible at work, such as the ability to manage information and appear detached and unemotional (depending upon your job), will appear less credible or less valuable at home, for example. The same behaviours there may be deemed to be wholly inappropriate. In some cases, no doubt, we could all be accused of still being at work because of the way we behave when we forget to change our behaviours.

But reduce your job to a series of behaviours, which would be needed in order that you survive in your post, and then simply imagine if you were given a completely different job elsewhere. How would you fare if you were moved from being a senior local government officer to being a bus driver? Equally, how would someone who was a bus driver fare in your office environment?

Put to one side the very specific knowledge needed to do your job and think for a moment about *excuses*. When we make an excuse about something we haven't done or something we have done badly, we ask others to continue to allow us to trade in the marketplace even though we have not delivered. So think for a moment what behaviours you can successfully employ when you make excuses that others, say from a different work background, could not use. Write those down and think for a moment about what makes them work. It could be said that excuses allow us to justify our inaction in ways which allow us to continue to maintain our credibility and, by looking at our excuses, this will give us some insight into the criteria which we use to award credibility in the first place.

If we accept that there are different credibility marketplaces we might want to think about what the criteria are for entry into each of them. One entry point might be the number of germane credible behaviours we are able to exhibit in that marketplace. One way of looking at this in practice is to look at the entry points into marketplaces.

Take a job selection process

For most staff in local government the way to employment is via a job interview. By closely examining the process we can look at how potential players (new employees) are able to demonstrate that they should be allowed to trade in the marketplace. The credibility marketplace, as with all markets, is underpinned by a relationship and so for a job selection process the marketplace consists of a local authority seeking to gain credibility with future employees and the employee seeking to gain it with the local authority as the potential employer.

The first filter will be the placing of an advertisement. It is not just for reasons of cost that we place advertisements in a select number of places. We advertise in places where we think potential employees will be. It is equally an exclusive action. We do not invite applicants from areas where we believe there will be no credible players. In the upper echelons of the church, or the legal profession, there is little market information available to anyone but those deemed to be credible. You don't see advertisements for High Court judges in *The Guardian*.

The advertisement itself will be worded to attract the appropriate individual. And while many advertisements will be written in a general sense (they are also an opportunity to position the employer with a wider audience) some will be written so that those who can't speak the language will not feel attracted. This might mean the inclusion of particular words or concepts.

Both the advertisement and the application pack will outline the next set of exclusion and inclusion criteria. It is said tritely that you can't get a job without experience and that you can't get experience without a job. It is at this point where this becomes the case. Here is the opportunity for the employer to determine the relevance of your experience and, although there is at last a trend towards competency-based job applications, there is still a tendency to determine experience on the basis of other credible activity. For example, applicants may be required to demonstrate five years' experience in a particular field rather than the acquisition of a number of skills and aptitudes during recent employment.

As the applicant is able to pass through each stage they accrue credibility. It might be as simple as:

- reading the right newspaper;
- understanding our language;
- being able to demonstrate success *in our terms.*

There are further means of testing credibility. We expect application forms to be clearly written (often typed) and grammatically correct with accurate spelling and so on. We may make a judgement about a person's credibility on factors which may have nothing to do with the job for which they are applying. People who suffer from dyslexia will know only too well how their apparent inability to spell can condition others' view of them as intellectually weak. The same applies to application forms. Accurate spelling may not be an important part of a person's particular occupation but it might be one way of reading that he or she may have a feckless attitude towards their work. Each credibility factor can be a metaphor for another.

This is best demonstrated in the job interview itself. We expect individuals to be able to muster the whole range of credible symbols to enter the marketplace. Some will be job-specific. If we were recruiting an accountant we would apply a set of professionally based criteria before awarding credibility. But alongside these there would be other credible behaviours which we would use as means of making overall judgements. American sociologist Erving Goffman (1959) has observed that we are more likely to make judgements about people on the basis of unintended remarks and actions than we are on the basis of planned actions. So the way that a candidate behaves in apparently spontaneous moments could be used to sustain a view about him or her in general. For example, we might expect a candidate for a post as a social worker to exhibit caring behaviour in all that they did during the period of the interview.

So at each point in the recruitment process candidates can be awarded credibility points. Without this peer group evaluation and acceptance they are less likely to make it through the process. Throughout each stage of this process we can imagine how a lack of credibility can be suggested and how dangerous that is to the possibility of gaining the job.

The same is true with the credibility of the local authority as a potential employer. The fact that they advertise in particular newspapers or magazines, and use the appropriate language, demonstrates to potential applicants an understanding of that particular marketplace. The pack about the job and their application form can be uninformative about the local authority or have no real questions which stretch the potential applicant. The interview can be a mess with different members of the interview board arguing with each other. They may not contact the successful applicant for some time, indicating that they cannot make decisions. All of these activities will diminish the credibility of the local authority in the eye of the potential employer.

In the next part of this chapter we look at whether there are a set of universal credible behaviours and symbols within our culture. If we do live in credibility marketplaces we must first acquire points before we can trade. In this section we also look at what behaviours, actions and symbols are credible. Finally, we look at how we might trade.

ACCUMULATING CREDIBILITY

Here we first outline the importance of four main criteria for gaining credibility:

- knowledge;
- wisdom;
- ways of behaving;
- the importance of symbols.

Knowledge

The acquisition of knowledge is prized in our culture. Those who know what they are talking about, the experts, are given weight by those who don't. We all, in one way or another, aspire to being an expert in some way or other. For senior local government managers it could simply be that you are the one who is good at putting together bidding documents. That you are recognized as an expert will be important in terms of your standing and status.

However, it is not simply knowledge in itself that matters. If that were so graduates joining local government with specialist qualifications would be among the most revered in the corridors of power and we all know that is not the case (although strangely, it takes a long while for new graduate recruits to learn this). There is more to expertise than knowing things. Another important feature is knowing how to apply knowledge and that is as much a product of experience as it is reading about how things are done. Again, experience is a prized commodity. Those who are able to apply their knowledge on the basis of how they know it is used will add points to their credibility rating.

But then not all knowledges are equal. If by knowledgeable we meant that someone was able to recount facts and demonstrate the application of knowledge then the doctor of medicine would stand alongside the pigeon-fancier. To most of us that is not the case. There is a hierarchy of knowledges. At the top of this hierarchy we will find bodies of knowledge which have been built over a period of years. Here you will find science, the law, philosophy and religion. In each of these the body of knowledge has been carefully crafted and guarded.

In science, for example, it is not enough to state that something is the case; it must be proved. In order for a fact to be the case in science it will have to have been tested against a number of criteria. Knowledge is added on the basis of appearance in credible publications. Journals such as *Nature*, for example, will, by virtue of having a board of knowledgeable experts, determine what is and is not the case.

In other bodies of knowledge there may be less stringent checks on what counts as fact. Where the knowledge body is less institutionalized then the knowledge will be less credible. Compare, for example, homeopathy with mainstream medicine.

Wisdom

Local government senior managers rarely deal with the same kind of problem repeatedly. Where a problem is known to exist and a solution found it is relatively easy to set up a process to ensure that it is handled in the same way each time it occurs. You need only look at the way that local government embraces new policy initiatives for working examples. When a policy priority is announced, such as on HIV and AIDS work, there will, following an initial period of best-practice sharing and networking, be a flurry of special officers specifically recruited into new posts with new titles. The system encourages the institutionalization of solutions.

Wisdom, though, is another matter. Wisdom is about knowing what the right form of action or inaction should be in a given set of circumstances. In local authorities, wisdom is also associated with political nous. Simply, it is unwise, in a political organization, to lack political nous.

It could be argued that the top jobs in local government are less to do with knowledge than they are with wisdom. Those who have wisdom must take account of a complex matrix of imperatives in order to reach a judgement. These include context, shared values, culture, knowing what others have done, thinking of outcomes and knowing the weight of the existing credibility and being able to draw on important received texts. In the end, their wisdom will allow them to make a judgement, which will inform actions leading to outcomes.

Context

This will involve an appraisal of the social, economic and political context within which the decision is to be made. Time is a factor here. A judgement on what it would have been appropriate for a senior male member of staff to say to a junior female member of staff 10 years ago would probably be different to the same circumstances today.

Shared values

It is possible to make assumptions about what is right and wrong in our society. Lest there be any doubt there are laws which remind us but we rarely refer to the statute books as a means of informing our opinions daily. We are more likely to simply know what is appropriate. Perhaps that is why so many of us rely on opinion-formers, the media and common sense to guide our thoughts. However, as we make decisions on a daily basis, we will receive feedback from others on our wisdom.

Culturally specific notions of right and wrong

These are likely to be rooted in the main in Christianity (although in a multi-cultural society new ways of understanding and judging will become part of our thinking processes). Again, it is by knowing (through reinforcement) the right way to do things here that we make judgements as to what is right or wrong.

Knowing what others have done

One clear test of the wisdom of our proposed action is to know what others have done in similar circumstances. At the least, it means that on the grounds of precedence we have a last line of defence. Much of our law stands on these pillars, but equally we know that others' judgements of the validity of our actions will also be made on this basis.

Thinking of the outcomes

In one sense this is the wisdom of Solomon. If we know that what might appear to be right might also result in the wrong outcome, and we know that the outcome would be one that others consider to be right, we might be more inclined to go with the wrong answer for the right reasons.

Knowing the weight of our existing credibility

The same action in the same circumstances can have completely different outcomes depending upon who takes the action. We consider the soundness of a judgement on the basis of the credibility of the decision-taker. Bound up in this is the idea that they should know better. The recent press flurry around the decoration bill for the Lord Chancellor's residence might, to some, have been concerned with whether he had exhibited sound judgement in his actions.

Ways of behaving

Most of what we learn about how to behave is a result of the interaction with our peers and colleagues at work. We know through experience and through, if necessary, codes of discipline what is acceptable behaviour. But while much of our behaviour will be habitual and idiosyncratic it is worth examining credible behaviour as a product of the power of particular individuals. It might be suggested that the sources of ways of behaving come down from above. That is, because local government is an aspirational organization with ambitious individuals hoping to rise through the ranks to higher paid posts, they will tend to mimic the habits of those above them as a means of being accepted.

One way, therefore, of signalling credibility might be to signal it through allusion to those in positions of power. Within each organization the idiosyncrasies of those in control will change. All the same, those in positions of power will need to signal to others that they are in such a position. Those who have more control over the work of others will be able to exert more control of their own personal space. In local authorities the ability to manage personal space will be one of the means by which others will read your status. In addition, it is still broadly the convention in local authorities that when a document goes to a committee it does so under the name of a particular chief officer, even though mostly junior officers will write the reports. This legitimates the role of the chief officer in determining the way it should be written and presented. It is another opportunity for a senior officer to determine what is credible. Within local government there is also a very specific issue of professional ways of behaving.

The importance of symbols

How do members signal to others about how they would expect to be treated? One way is through the use of forms of credible behaviours which are associated with high-status professions. If you wanted to signal that you were articulate then it is likely you would use:

- good sentence constructions;
- a strong vocabulary;
- appropriate use of pauses in speaking;
- confident cueing – where you signal to the other person when to speak.

Similarly, if you wished to signal that you were intelligent, you might refer to books or publications which are deemed to be in the domain of intelligent people (because they may be written in a language which is complex and specialized). You might say 'this argument was well-rehearsed in Hugo Young's column last week but even he recognized the importance of Von Klauswitz's analysis of war'. The use of such techniques is shorthand for saying 'I am an intelligent person and you should take me seriously'.

One of the important symbols is the way in which we present ourselves through dress. In some places of work this will mean do they wear a uniform and if they do are they wearing it in the right way? Some employers will specify exactly how an employee is to dress but in local government, save for certain front-line staff, officers rarely have to wear a uniform.

However, the absence of specific forms of dress offers no more freedom. Officers will learn that suits, broadly conservative and classical, will be the desired dress. For men it means a shirt, tie and matching shoes. It could be suggested that in choosing what to dress in we rely on other accepted forms of dress. It may be that what we wear alludes to uniform and since we know that uniforms are acceptable and respectable ways of dressing we will benefit from the credibility by association.

Of course, uniforms do not work for everybody. While in the services we might expect everybody to wear the same kinds of uniform, personnel will still need some form of differentiation. In the services different ranks will wear different epaulettes and the like as a means of marking out their territory but in local authorities such distinctions are less obvious. By and large uniforms tend to be restricted to manual staff. Senior officers must, therefore, find other ways of badging themselves in order that others know their rank.

Symbols are powerful ways of short-circuiting the process of conveying meaning. When the Local Government Association (LGA) was created it was believed that the organization should try to establish itself quickly. The LGA's corporate identity was one key way of conveying that message.

Case study: 'Developing a corporate identity for the LGA', by Carol Grant, former Director of Communications and Public Affairs

When I became Director of Communications at the Local Government Association, six months before its launch in April 1998, one of my first jobs was to develop and implement a new corporate identity. Symbols are important – they define an organization. This was a new merged body with a longer gestation period than an elephant, and plenty of critics who would be quick to seize on mistakes. It was something I couldn't afford to get wrong.

I was lucky – no one seriously suggested getting it done on the cheap. However, it does amaze me that there are still those in local government who subscribe to the 'let's get the local schoolchildren to design a logo' syndrome. Try suggesting that next time they go for a job interview they get their suits made by the local needlework class.

So I had a budget, but time and money were tight. This was a problem, and also an opportunity. Deadlines forced me to find creative short cuts. Lean budgets meant I had to get people to focus on what they really wanted. Being a strategically important client helped – a range of top design companies pitched for the work, and did it within a tight budget because they saw the value of the LGA on their client list. The process itself was helping to define us as a key player in the field.

When I arrived, the brief had already been written – by committee! It was the product of three organizations coming together, somewhat reluctantly. But the brief had to reflect a brand new, whole, organization, not a collection of parts held in place with Sellotape. So I rewrote the brief, based on what I, as a newcomer and as a communications professional, saw as the key selling points of the new organization. Deadlines concentrate the mind wonderfully – if people thought differently, they were able to shout, but quickly.

The brief set out the background to the formation of the LGA, and described how it would work. It outlined the aims and core values (taken from documents already produced). It set out the requirements that the new symbol should reflect the LGA as:

- a brand new body, not simply a successor;
- having status and influence with government and decision-makers;
- having a public service ethos and being democratic and accountable;
- being modern and dynamic;
- being inclusive and speaking for local communities as a whole;
- operating on a cross-party, consensual basis.

The symbol had to be durable, but also be capable of adaptation in future. We also wanted it to be capable of being used as a more generic symbol for local government as a whole.

There were also practical requirements – it couldn't resemble any of the political parties' symbols, either in colour or design. It had to be identifiable in domestic, European and international contexts, and be capable of being customized by the different regional and special interest groups within the LGA. It needed to be easily read by people with a visual impairment, be cost-effective and environmentally friendly.

The design and selection process was an inclusive one, involving both staff and members. There is nothing more subjective than a symbol to capture the essence of an organization, and the choice is a very personal issue. In working with designers, I found their intuitive understanding of the organization, and their willingness to share in where it was going, was as important as any technical ability.

Staff were given the chance to comment on a short-list of designs, and their comments, and mine, went forward to a panel of councillors. They chose the winner – the 'star people', designed by a company called HSAG. One councillor explained her decision by saying she 'needed to think about how those out there in the backwoods will see this symbol'. My heart sank – by nature I am more inclined to favour the pioneers than the backwoodsmen, but she was right. This was a new organization with a troubled birth. It was their political organization, not mine. The symbol needed to be something that 22 000 councillors out there could unite around, challenging enough to be distinctive while familiar enough to be comfortable.

People seldom remember the genesis of a symbol, but for the record, the star people logo represented a number of things:

- Shaped like England and Wales, the LGA's constituency, it conveyed an upward, positive movement.

- Its star-shaped figures conveyed that people, both within local communities and councils themselves, are the stars of local government.
- The stars gave it a European, devolved feeling.
- The strong magenta colour gave it a non-political, contemporary feel.

There was no adverse reaction to the image itself – it was universally praised. What criticism there was centred on the magenta colour, somewhat unkindly described by then local government minister David Curry as 'boudoir pink' at its launch in January 1997. But the primary colour, and the palette of secondary colours used alongside (mainly lime-green and tomato) were modern and funky, and lifted the image into another league. That year, everyone at the cutting-edge of design was using those colours. They weren't typically local government, but they were what people saw in supermarkets, clothes shops, building societies, clubs, in fact, anywhere they went about their daily business. As a positioning tool to put local government at the heart of people's lives, it worked.

Introducing the logo in January, in advance of the LGA's launch in April, was important. It allowed us to build recognition of the new look on basic materials while ironing out more complex applications later. It also allowed for lots of mini-launches of associated products, because the development of the symbol was part of a bigger corporate makeover – new looks for magazines, publications, electronic communication and more. It was all about saying – we're different, and distinctive.

The image itself was also flexible and fun. People liked the star people analogy. At the first annual conference 'A Brighter Future' in July 1997, the symbol was used in stage design and reinforced by the conference title and the use of 'Satellite Sessions' to describe workshops. The symbol was even reworked into a star people Christmas tree for the LGA's first Christmas card!

Was it successful? An unqualified yes. Many people commented to me over the course of the first year that it was the best corporate identity they could have hoped for. A MORI survey of LGA members found that its biggest single strength was seen to be in promoting a positive image of local government. The little symbol certainly played a starring role in that achievement!

TRADING IN THE CREDIBILITY MARKETPLACE

If we accept the existence of the credibility marketplace, and we accept that there are a number of means of signalling credibility, then it must be possible to learn to trade. However, trading is not simply the manipulation of behaviours and symbols. In local government, we must also recognize the importance of integrity – the need to acquire relevant knowledge and the development of sound judgement – for these are at the heart of our credibility not only in work but also in society at large. The exercise of keeping your credibility under review can be important in itself as a check on how effectively others think you are performing. Worcestershire County Council, following training carried out with their chief officers, now regularly review their credibility rating. While such an approach won't give you a total picture of how others see you, it will give you another insight.

But let's be clear about what we mean by trading in credibility. In practical terms this is about recognizing that in the new local government, officers will need to be able to establish and maintain credibility with a number of different audiences. In *Leading the Way*, the Prime Minister, Tony Blair (Blair, 1997), made it clear that local government had failed to meet its customers on anything like equal terms. There was, and remains, a failure to involve, to engage and to communicate. What's more, in the post-municipal world, local government will need to seek out and establish partnerships as a means of providing services to local people. If local authorities are to be able to engage the community then they must be capable of being taken seriously by all of the different elements within each community.

That will mean being as credible to businesspeople as it will to bingo halls. If there was a time when local government officers could rely upon their title to give them *gravitas* at public meetings, that time, for most of the country, has long gone. There are clear signs that the local democratic mandate is being eroded. It will be incumbent upon officers and members to rebuild trust with local communities and that means understanding what deems them credible and believable in the eyes of those local people and using that knowledge for the positive benefit of the community.

How then should we begin to trade? These are the main themes:

- taking stock;
- knowing your shareholders;
- thinking about the defining moments of credibility;
- being aware of your value in the marketplace;
- giving people a chance to invest in the future;
- building a method of measuring the return in the marketplace;
- developing newer techniques to trade in the market.

Taking stock

Before you set about seeking to establish your credibility you must first know how credible you are deemed to be. The best way of gathering this information is through a third party. If, for example, you are a senior environmental officer who must build trust with local businesses it would be folly to ask your customers or clients what they thought of you. It is vital that you have unpolluted information which will tell you what people think. Some authorities use 360 degree appraisals. These can provide valuable, frank and incredibly helpful data. They will tell you not only about how others see you but also why they have the view they do.

It is vital to know what things matter to your clients. Is it important that you are polite? Or punctual? Or efficient? In the ideal world, what kind of people would they want to deal with? You need to know what matters to them. In other words, when you are seeking to find out what they think of you, you need to allow yourself to be seen in their terms.

How has your stock been over recent years? How many unfulfilled promises will your community or key publics remember? What will you do to repair the damage left by that?

And, of course, if you are a manager the value of your stock depends also upon the credibility of the people who work for you. It is almost as if you have an assets portfolio with other members of staff, all trading in your interests in different marketplaces. You will need to know how they are trading. You will need to look at whether their stock is rising or falling. And, before you give tasks to particular members of staff, you will need to be clear about whether they will be deemed credible in that particular marketplace.

Knowing your shareholders

If community governance is to mean anything it surely must mean that everyone in a community has a stake in the future. With them, you, as the local authority, will articulate what the future will look like, but it will be in you that they invest. You control many of the resources – the time, the money and the energy – which will make that future possible. If you've made promises in the past and haven't delivered they will be less willing to invest. The low electoral turnouts of recent years must, in some way, be an indication that local people have overinvested and are not prepared to invest any more unless they see a return on what they've put in so far. However, if people are to believe in your authority they need to know that you understand their concerns, share their problems and are committed to their ends.

In essence, it is unlikely that the public will continue to invest by taking part in elections, for example, where they feel that you are not yet delivering the promises you have already made. So it will be vital that you are aware of the outstanding promises made by the authority. Further, to what extent are you dealing with the needs of individual members of the public? Local government is in a very difficult position. Inevitably, you can't please everyone all of the time. So you will need to know what impact the disappointed will have on your general market credibility value. For example, if you make a public promise to the head of the local chamber of commerce and then fail to deliver, that could have more impact on your share value than a disappointed council taxpayer whose bin collection remains on a Bank Holiday collection day.

Thinking about the defining moments of credibility

The way that you as an individual officer or your authority manages crunch points will determine how others see you. When you attend meetings how do you conduct yourself? Are you polite? When you chair meetings do you allow everyone to have a say? When you meet with members of the community do you listen? Do you respond? Do you appear to understand their concerns?

Are you clear what the defining moments are in your authority? Are they the Audit Commission performance indicators? Or do your publics have other important indicators? Have you asked your customers recently what things *actually matter to them*? It may be that answering the phone within three rings, for example, is less important than the person being able to help when they do answer the phone.

Once you know what the defining moments are then you can start to think about how you deal with them. Schools will, for example, shape parents' perceptions often on the basis of how they manage occasions such as the first day at school, exclusions, exam results and parents' evenings. Critically, if you are to appear credible to others you need to consider how you appear to them.

Being aware of your value in the marketplace

How often do you find out exactly what people think of your authority? Or of you as an officer or member? Many authorities now carry out resident attitude surveys. These can be a useful way of taking stock but since they are generally infrequent (every one to two years) they will be less useful as a means of informing your trading on a week-by-week basis. While it is important to have landmarks it is now information that will tell you if you are losing weight within your community.

There is no short-cut. It's a question of keeping an ear to the ground, carrying out regular research on user perceptions on an ongoing basis and being willing to listen to uncomfortable truths.

What about the last time where was a public flotation – the election. Here, through voting, the authority asked local people to publicly invest their trust in another person. What was the turnout like? Did you carry out an exit poll to find out what part of the community still appears to believe in the process? What do you know of the issues that conditioned their decision to vote?

What about recent public meetings or complaints? Any information about what the people in your marketplace think is valuable. Does your authority regularly consider it? Do you change your behaviour as a result of consistent complaints? Do you check with complainants to see whether they are any happier now with your ways of behaving?

Giving people a chance to invest in the future

Short-term thinking will damage long-term credibility. We know from the stock market that a company can continue to trade, even though it may have been in the red for a number of years, provided their shareholders believe that things will get better.

Have you given your shareholders a reason to believe? Have you helped them build a single conception of the future or have you been changing your mind, jumping from one project to the next, never fully completing anything and never letting your shareholders know whether their investment has been worth while.

Local authorities often set out their views on the way ahead in terms of a vision or mission statement. If you have one, were local people involved in putting it together? Is there any evidence that they either understand or believe it? Is it easy to show your customers how they can measure the return they might be getting on their investment of trust in you? It might simply be that they are able to perceive changes in the quality of your relationships rather than any additional investments.

Building a method of measuring the return in the marketplace

While most authorities rejected performance indicators as meaningless and counterproductive one thing they did do was tune local people into the idea that you can know how well you are doing. If performance indicators fail to address the local perspective, change them so that they meet local needs for information and help you work with your community to establish what success would look like. If they invest their trust in you, they and you will need to know whether it has been worth while.

Developing newer techniques to trade in the market

In an earlier section we mentioned the importance of third-party endorsements. So it can be with your communities. If you are to win credibility within the various communities you serve, you will need to be winning support among those whose views already matter there – local opinion-formers. Some authorities have been very effective in winning support from community key opinion-formers. Others have appeared tokenistic. While that might appear to have the veneer of involvement it may undermine the credibility of the authority.

In the stock market the FTSE is made up of the market values of a number of key stocks and shares. Should we not adopt a similar approach to measuring the credibility of the local authority? Imagine, for example, that your local authority regularly took the views of say 20 key players in your area. You might choose the following group of people in the following exercise:

 Exercise – credibility in the marketplace

a local church person (A);
a local policeman (B);
a customer panel drawn from each of your wards (C);
a journalist (D);
a local primary and secondary headteacher (E);
a number of randomly chosen customers (F);
a local businessperson (G);
an academic (H);
a member of each political party in the area (I).

You might ask each person the following questions:

On a scale of 0–10, where 0 is no belief and 10 is total belief, how would you rate the authority on its:

- ability to deliver its promises?
- the quality of its services?
- its judgement on the following decisions (...)?
- the quality of its customer care?
- its ability to listen to your point of view?
- its interest in involving you in decision-making?

The following Table 1.1 illustrates how this might work.

You would then accumulate the score and this would be one part of your *credibility rating*. The second part would be a *general rating* on how optimistic the audiences felt. It would act as a multiplier. This might be akin to the general feel-good that exists (or doesn't) in the city of London. If traders feel that life ahead is both predictable and positive then shares would be generally trading up. If life was predictable and negative shares might trade down. However, if life was unpredictable then that might cause shares to trade down anyway.

Table 1.1 Calculating credibility

	A	B	C	D	E	F	G	H	I
Ability to deliver its promises?	5	5	6	1	8	5	4	2	7
The quality of its services?	2	7	8	6	4	5	7	6	4
Its judgement on the following decisions (…)?	4	5	1	6	6	7	1	2	2
The quality of its customer care?	7	7	5	7	7	6	3	8	7
Its ability to listen to your point of view?	4	2	6	1	3	5	2	4	4
Its interest in involving you in decision-making?	2	2	4	2	4	5	4	5	4
Totals	24	28	30	23	32	33	21	27	28

Similarly, you could have a *general rating* which would be dependent upon *local conditions.* If there were no plans to cut services, or raise council tax and the council was fulfilling its promises, then you might apply a *general rating of* 1.25. People would feel optimistic. The overall score would be multiplied by 1.25. On the other hand, people might be worried about the impact of government cuts on local services and that, coupled with uncertainty over a coming local election, might cause people to feel uncertain. The *general rating* might be 0.75.

Table 1.2 The credibility rating

Group	Rating
A	24
B	28
C	30
D	23
E	32
F	33
G	21
H	27
I	28
Total	246
Multiplier general rating	1.15
Total (246×1.15)	282.9

In this exercise your credibility rating would be 282.9.

You could carry out this test on a monthly basis and use it to inform your current standing in the marketplace. You could be more specific and test how individual decisions are seen. It would be critical to have a consistent measure. In the absence of regular, objective data, there is a danger that other forms of measurement will dominate. How many decisions, for example, are skewed by what is being said in your local paper or how many decisions are affected by the timing of the electoral cycle?

By adopting such a measure your authority could easily benchmark its performance against other local authorities using similar measures. What's more, it would give the council benchmarks against which it could compare performance inside the authority. This is critical if local authorities are to move their thinking on improving service beyond the fear and blame-driven systems that dominate so many councils.

Such a process is important not just for a whole authority, but for each part of each authority. Every middle manager can work out their own credibility rating, that of their staff and that of the service they provide. Middle managers also trade in the credibility marketplace, and can gain and lose in that marketplace. It is vital to check regularly on your credit rating in credibility, not as some academic exercise, but as a process of improvement and a method of increasing your capacity to manage in the new local government. The next chapter looks much more closely at how individuals can manage their own reputations.

2 Personal positioning – do these glasses really make me look like Cary Grant?

Where the first chapter talked about how authorities' reputations can be made or broken on the basis of what they do, this chapter looks at how individuals shape others' perceptions. It examines the idea of 'branding' and how an essentially commercial term can be used to understand the way that people and local authorities are seen. It then looks at how branding techniques can be used to enable us all to be seen differently by those we deal with. Next I will focus on the idea of developing a personal positioning strategy – a way of deliberately setting out to be seen in a particular way. Finally, I will look at how to use event-management thinking to manage ways in which others might see us.

Before you can get anything serious done in a management post you need to be taken seriously by your staff. Strong managers know that the title of 'manager' alone will help you get very little done in any senior post. What's more, those who rely on status or position to convince colleagues of a particular course of action do little more than undermine their own authority, since their staff and colleagues quickly recognize their title being used as their sole authority – a strategy that quickly wears out. Those who succeed in management positions are, by and large, those who are able to lead their staff. Further, they will be people who will help others develop and grow to meet the challenges that their part of the organization faces.

Alongside this, it's worth remembering that there are very few charismatic people in the world. Those that have that characteristic may not turn to management to use it, and if they do few turn to public service management. You won't find too many people like Richard Branson in local government's corridors of power. You will find them but they're thin on the ground. However, the characteristics that the likes of Branson display are not beyond the wit of most middle managers to learn and use effectively.

This chapter is concerned with how managers can position themselves so that they are better placed to win the support of their staff. It suggests that this can be achieved by seeing yourself in a new way – as a brand – rather than simply as a person. It's not a new idea. All of us consume branded products on a daily basis. It is partly because we believe that the TSB is a bank *that likes to say 'yes'* that we bank there or we will be attracted by the clinical and medical feel of Boots the Chemist that helps us wander into their shops as opposed to cheaper alternatives. And few of us, who have the choice, will have Tesco jeans in our wardrobes as long as Wrangler and Levis are on the market. Whereas we might associate Tesco with cheap, good quality family shopping (and Dame Shirley Porter) we would rarely ascribe to it the sorts of qualities we like to see in our jeans. It takes a fertile imagination to visualize the sexually driven images that sell the brand of Levis when we walk into the nearest supermarket. However, it would be wrong to think that such a set of images is not a major part of what we buy in jeans.

Branding is the art of attributing specific qualities which are not inherent in products to those products. If we were to describe products in generic terms – that is what they actually appear to be – the meaning of those products would be quite different from the perceived meaning that they would have as brands. So a pair of jeans could simply be a pair of canvas trousers, which may be coloured blue, with studs for additional reinforcement on all of the pockets. However, when you think Levis that description will rarely enter your head.

If you are a company establishing an identity for your brand you will attribute certain qualities to it. This can be done through advertising where, through repetition, it is possible to associate particular images, or music or words with a particular product. It can also be done through association where companies are able to use existing products and align them with their new product in the hope that the attributes will somehow transfer.

Of course, it's not an exact science. For example, a company launching a new pension plan might ask the previous Chancellor of the Exchequer, Nigel Lawson, to be associated with it. To some Nigel Lawson would have the Iron Chancellor image to his credit and in the context of a financial package that might be a useful attribute. However others, thinking of him politically, might simply associate him with the Conservative Party and depending upon whether they were supporters might take a positive or a negative view.

And it could go on. Nigel Lawson's daughter is a journalist (Nigella). Her increase in visibility – she can be seen regularly on chat shows and the like – might overshadow her father and there may be a different association there. Or, since he has written a popular book on the subject, we might these days associate slimming with him. In this case he represents a different set of images and cannot simply be associated with one clutch of meanings. Companies who use association techniques would want to know what attributes their possible choice might have with the particular audience they are trying to reach.

Companies might also merchandise their products to reinforce the essential messages. This would involve placing the products in certain sorts of stores and with certain sorts of packaging. In recent years Calvin Klein has tried to stop Tesco from selling their clothes in their supermarkets since this form of merchandising would confuse their image, and this confused image would confuse the message about their product. So companies try and keep a tight hold on how their goods are directly presented to the public in the marketplace.

Branding though is not simply a matter of advertising and merchandising. It is important that the product itself delivers some of the qualities that have been ascribed to it. Levis are tough but no tougher than other brands of jeans, but if they were less tough than other jeans there would be a problem for the brand.

Another way in which attributes can be ascribed to products is in the way that consumers themselves do so. When you buy Levi jeans you buy into a particular way of seeing them. That is, of course, reinforced through a continuous stream of advertising, but if they can get you to believe that when you smoke Marlborough you are somehow the 'Marlborough Man' because you smoke them, then you will help reinforce their brand, both in your own mind and in those of the people you associate with. Your friends and colleagues may refer to the brands you use as a means of describing you.

SELF AS BRAND

The same range of methods can be applied to managers in local government. That's not to suggest that we should all rush out and commission advertising campaigns to promote ourselves. That's not what companies do to brand their products. Rather, we can use this way of seeing to think about how others inside and outside the local authority might see us. The next section is about how to think of yourself as a form of brand and how to position yourself as the kind of manager you might want to be. If you promote the idea that you are a caring, sharing manager who always puts the needs of your staff first, if your behaviour consistently says that and if your staff say that about you then that's what you are. And when they talk to other people about you that's how you will be presented. As previously mentioned this can only work if it goes beyond appearance into the reality of how you work. The crucial issue is consistency.

However, when other people talk about you they may only say it now and again. You will need an overall strategy to position yourself as a manager within and outside the organization. Personal positioning strategy is concerned with spreading that message about the way in which you actually manage more widely and about finding and pruning those descriptions that may be used about you which undermine those particular brand values.

Establishing your brand

When was the last time you were brutally honest about the kind of person you really are? If you've ever done it then you are brave, for criticism is one of the things that most of us fear more than anything else. Perhaps it is because appraisals are precisely about asking uncomfortable questions about how people do relate to one another that they are fretted over. There is, however, no alternative to this honest appraisal and it simply needs to be done. If you cannot be honest about yourself and how others see you, it is not possible to change.

Developing a personal positioning strategy means working through a number of stages. These are:

- defining yourself;
- asking others to define you (or knowing how they do);
- deciding how you want to be perceived;
- defining your new position through key messages, defining moments, opinion-formers and actions.

STAGE ONE – DEFINE YOURSELF

This is not about trekking off to the foothills of the Himalayas and living barefoot in a cult. It's about being clear about how you want to be seen. What kind of beast are you? This is never really an easy question to answer but there are a number of ways to get at the answer. One way is to write down a list of what you think your key qualities are – single words would be enough. You might, for example, write: 'warm', 'caring' and 'open'. You could divide the list into two and, admitting that not all qualities will be positive, have a negative column, too. But don't exclude certain words because they make you feel uncomfortable.

Another method is to use a lateral thinking tool. Imagine that you are a car and then try to write down what kind of car you would be. Again, a two-column approach might give you more useful data. In column one you could say what you would be, in column two you could say why. For example, 'I would be a Morris Minor because it is quaint, individualistic and has rare qualities'. However, even if you only ever show yourself the answers, do it properly. It is impossible to carry out this task without being honest.

STAGE TWO – ASK OTHERS TO DEFINE YOU

This is a less easy stage to complete since it always begs the question, 'why do you want to know?'. If you are going to seriously work through this exercise it might be better to find a close friend (because you might not like what you are hearing) to do this for you. Just as above you could apply the same questions, writing down what specific words people would use to describe you. To help you and your close friend to make these judgements it may be worth while carrying out a simple test.

What do you think they would do?

This is simply about getting people to speculate about what others might do in a particular set of circumstances. You would then use that information to get comments on how people feel you might behave. The hope is that in giving you an answer the person you are speaking to will give you some sort of justification for their response.

One easy route into the question is to describe a situation that you or someone else you know found themselves in and pose it as a dilemma. It's a 'I-wasn't-really-sure-what-to-do' thing. By suggesting that you, and hopefully they, would find it difficult you then ask what they think others (including the person you are gathering information on) might have done.

For example: the Leader caught me on the hop today. He came in while I was writing a short memo to the Leader of the Opposition. I felt really embarrassed when he asked me what I was doing. I have to say I shuffled around awkwardly and changed the subject. What would you have done?

(They answer.) What do you think so and so would have done? And then probe for more detail.

If this process is to work effectively then you need absolute honesty. There is little point in pretending that people understand you as one kind of person when in fact they really believe you are quite a different person. This stage is essentially a position and it is vital that you find out as much as possible about what others think of you.

STAGE THREE – DECIDE HOW YOU WANT TO BE PERCEIVED

Given a blank sheet a great many of us would want to have charisma, star quality and the rest. However, unless you have the base material of the likes of Robert Redford, no matter what you do you will never end up looking like him. Many authorities, in going through Investors in People, have defined what good management and good managers are and if you are going to maximize your impact as a manager that should really be your starting point. Remember why you are there. Your job as a manager is to help muster resources in the most effective and efficient way to deliver what the council wants.

So it would be worth gathering in data which tells you how your staff want you to operate. The chances are that it will be open, honest, involving, able to manage fairly and so on.

Are you up to it?

If managers are not prepared to admit that they are the right person for the job then there will always be a block in the system. If, however, people are prepared to admit their strengths and weaknesses then they can be better placed within the system. Different groups of people will work better under different styles of management but such diversity will not be able to be employed unless managers admit first that it exists.

In examining what your particular strengths are you should be looking to best package what you really are. A manager who is a naturally caring person will tend to feel uncomfortable where they present themselves as a hard-edged individual. The opposite is also true. However, where you are able to present your key attributes as part of a consistent face then you are more likely to be taken as you really are. Pretending to be something we are not is difficult to sustain but once we are clear about what we are – what our strengths and weaknesses are – we will be in a better position to behave in ways which support rather than contradict that definition.

How do you want to be seen? What kind of manager do you really want to be considered to be? Begin this stage by writing down the words which, if you are successful, will be used by others to describe you. However, bear in mind two things: what you bring to the equation – the kind of person you are; and how you are currently perceived.

It may be that you are a kind, considerate and caring person but you might be perceived to be a brutal, ruthless and manipulative person who simply uses caring language to get what you want. If that is the case it will be difficult to change the way that people see you quickly. It may be, because of the history of your relationships that, short of moving house, job or country, you will never get there. Some things we have done in the past will continue to define who we are today because they were particularly strong actions. We may get close to them, understand them, even think they have changed but the way in which we see them is likely to be affected by those past strong actions. Most of our past, though, is not like that, and has not left such a powerful image. We can rework it.

STAGE FOUR – DEFINING YOUR NEW POSITION

Specifically, there are four elements:

- key messages;
- defining moments;
- using opinion-formers;
- determining which actions will be important.

Key messages

A key message, in this context, is a phrase which may be used over and over again to describe an individual. It is important in terms of the ways in which others perceive that person.

Your position audit (stage two) should have given you an insight into the messages that are currently attached to you. It's worth recognizing that messages or labels are easily attached to individuals and, depending upon the person ascribing them, may rarely be challenged. This is for two reasons. First, it is easier to take statements about others at face value. We could spend hours examining one sentence used to describe another. Indeed, the legal system will do just that when the description is tied in some way with a crime. The ways that various people have described President Clinton are rarely open to serious public scrutiny and yet they often form part of the way that we see him when reported by the media.

The second point concerns the power of opinion-formers to shape our perceptions of others. A number of individuals in our society have the power to define others. When we apply for a job, we invite such ascription. We ask significant others (people who will be believed) to define us to other people. In a local authority a number of people automatically have the right to label you. These are:

- your immediate superior;
- councillors;
- senior officers;
- clients or customers.

When you define your key messages you will need to take into account the way that people speak, and the evidence that people will need to see in order to believe that you are as you say you are. You will also need to think about the kinds of behaviour you would normally associate with those kinds of messages. Be clear about the ways in which you would want others to describe you. Write those phrases down in the language that others would use in conversation.

Defining moments

In the previous section I talked about the importance of what people say about you as well as the role of opinion-formers or leaders but it is not always possible to cultivate those relationships. Sometimes, there simply aren't the opportunities. This section looks at how we can make maximum use of set piece occasions, or defining moments, to manage our own impressions as a means of presenting ourselves in a particular light.

Think of the key events in your life. The most obvious will be job interviews, family occasions, presentations to key groups or first day in a new job. Because of the complexity of such events we may be inclined to believe the impression of others which we perceive on those occasions. So even though we may think that someone may be 'good at interviews' we know that they won't know much about the panel, or the questions they may be asked, and so we may be inclined to see such occasions as ways of 'seeing people for what they are'. That is why, from an impression management point of view, defining moments are critical. If believability and attention increases and we are able to manage the way we represent ourselves then we will be able to add weight to a particular definition of ourselves. In short, we can shape others' perceptions of us.

However, defining moments are crucial for another reason – they are one-off. You only get one chance at a job interview. If you are unsuccessful, your prospective employer will not phone you up the next day and allow you to try again. And if you think of the number of separate people, resources and planning processes that converge on your wedding, it's easy to see why if you don't get it right, it can leave a powerful and negative lasting impression.

In all probability most of us will be pleased with the way our wedding went. We know that certain relatives won't have spoken since they argued, or even fought, at the last wedding. We may know that the hotel wasn't the best in the world but we also had time to let people know that the food would be 'wholesome' rather than 'anything flash' and so on. The reason weddings work is because of the amount of planning and prior knowledge which key individuals put into them. It is precisely because they have been given a project manager, a budget, an understanding of the potential pitfalls and both resources and time to overcome any difficulties that they are a success. In short, they have been treated as events and they have been managed and time and effort have gone into their planning.

The other defining moments in your life are no less important. Why then do we leave so much to chance? In the final part of the chapter we look at how to use event management thinking to manage impressions.

However, as you read through this chapter, think what defining moments are important to you, which are important in terms of the way you judge others and which others will use to judge you. These may simply be the way that you behave when you go to a committee meeting or when you present yourself to your management teams. Write them down and keep them in mind when you are thinking about how you want to be seen by others.

Using opinion-formers

Opinion-formers are people to whom we look to help us clarify our opinions about things. We may, in search of clarity on our views, simply lift others' opinions and make them our own. This is more likely to be the case where we have little or no personal experience of the matter under question. In those cases we are likely to rely on the word of others who appear to know what is going on. Generally speaking we form many of our opinions from the media. After all, we don't really know what is going on but others, who are better informed, can help us reach a view and if asked for an opinion on most things most of us would probably not want to admit that we have no view. In those circumstances we simply import the views of others.

In a work setting there will be those who find themselves in a similar authoritative position. It may be that your director or chief officer appears to be in the know. There will be others – trade union representatives, other chief officers, powerful politicians and so on. Opinion-formers are important both in terms of how they shape the context within which things have meaning where you work and in society in general. However, as far as personal positioning is concerned they will also be able to express a view about you or your team. Their words will carry weight and if they reinforce the way in which you want to be seen then you are more likely to be seen that way.

There are a number of stages through which you should go in order to use opinion-formers to help your positioning strategy. These are:

- selecting opinion-formers on the basis of whether they can help progress your positioning;
- understanding the opinion-former's agenda;
- understanding how that might relate to what you want to achieve;
- making yourself visible, tangible and useful;
- reducing the way you describe yourself to simple messages.

Selecting opinion-formers on the basis of whether they can help progress your positioning

In any set of circumstances there will be a number of opinion-formers but your choice will depend upon which audiences you need to reach with your new positioning statement. For example, if you wanted your department to be seen differently by a number of senior councillors it would be important to select an opinion-former to whom they looked for views and comment. It could be that positive comments made about your department by the leader of the council would cause others to take his or her word for it. It would be a third-party endorsement of your position but that endorsement would only count if the person doing so mattered to the audience you were trying to reach.

Understanding the opinion-former's agenda

In order to get someone else to say something positive about you it is worth establishing what *they* are trying to achieve. In any working environment achieving outcomes is often the result of a number of transactions or deals. In short, people need help to get things done and if you are in a position to provide support it will help others think better of you. If you are hoping to get an opinion-former to say something that will help your positioning strategy, you will first need to understand what they would want out of the transaction. You might want to think about the skills or understanding that you have of events which might be of help to that person. Simply put: once someone can understand how you might be able to help them they might be more inclined to help you.

Understanding how that might relate to what you want to achieve

In the business of getting favours in the bank (though they would never be referred to as such) you will need to remain focused. It is vital that those opinion-formers with whom you are forming productive relationships are actually in a position to help. Think through the best and worst circumstances. In the best circumstances they will pass on positive messages (hopefully your messages) about you to other audiences you need to reach. In the worst circumstances they may do the opposite – say that you're not what you claim to be – or simply say nothing. It is vital that you stay focused on achieving your outcome but in order to be able to do so you will need to cross-reference what that person wants against what you want. If there is an overlap then you can do business. If there is no overlap then you may well be wasting your time.

Making yourself visible, tangible and useful

If you choose to enlist an opinion-former they will need to know you are there. Visibility will be important. But, moreover, once visible they will also need to recognize in you the answer to some of their problems. Any meetings will have to be carefully considered and engineered. One management consultant interviewed regarding this strategy talked about creating as many opportunities as possible to discuss business with important opinion-formers in a particular marketplace. In his case that meant everything from passing on useful articles through to convening short meetings to clarify thinking. This might seem unwelcome but when you consider the difficulty of the agenda facing senior managers in local government the enlightened self-interest of capable others might be welcome.

However, these productive, symbiotic relationships must be handled very carefully. In approaching an opinion-former you will need to have credibility with that person. In Chapter 1 we focused on ways of accumulating credibility management but if someone is to invest their trust and judgement in you it will be important that you demonstrate that you are worth investing in.

Reducing the way you describe yourself to simple messages

None of us has much time for detail. We like simplicity in the main and we like to be able to easily understand the world around us. It helps if we can reduce others to simple descriptions and pigeonhole them and it is because of our desire to do so that we are able to originate those descriptions about ourselves and pass them on to others. Be clear: if we don't affect the nature of those descriptions they will be originated by others.

Once you have developed productive relationships with others think about the ways in which you would want them to describe you and then find ways of introducing these descriptions into your conversation. You might use humour or you might use passing remarks. In order that your messages become currency about you they will need to be simple, oft-repeated and consistent.

Determining which actions will be important

The final part of positioning strategy is the most important as ultimately it is not what people say about us that matters; it is what we do. Our actions will always speak much louder than the words used to describe us. Crucially, if we want to be seen to be a particular kind of person we must become that person. In one sense personal positioning strategy will help us get there more quickly or help focus our image but none of these things will have any long-term effect unless we act in the same way.

Others will already hold a view about what kind of person you would need to be to be described in any way. We are likely to believe, rightly or wrongly, that people who work in the caring professions should be caring. We believe that senior company executives are ruthless, financially-driven and cold and so on. If we are to change the perceptions that others hold because of stereotypes we would be foolish to ignore their preconceptions but because of the power of those preconceptions it is all the more important that our actions speak as loudly as our words.

It is vital that you consider what actions you will have to take on a regular and sustained basis in order to make your performance real. Ultimately the reality you create must have integrity if it is to be taken seriously.

In the final part of this chapter we look at how defining moments can be managed in the same way as any organized event. If we accept that actions are important it is worth considering, if we are to achieve our new position quickly and efficiently, which actions we should perform first. Which actions will others remember and comment upon? Which actions are important to you? You might want to consider, if you are seeking to change others' opinions of you, which actions would make the most difference to the way they see you.

MANAGING DEFINING MOMENTS THROUGH EVENT MANAGEMENT

Think of any event that must be managed carefully. There are a number of elements. This section takes each element in turn and looks at ways in which it can be applied to your day-to-day behaviour. The elements are as follows:

- define the event;
- decide on the desired outcomes;
- define the audience;
- gather all market information;
- decide what kind of impact you want to create (including the five senses);
- decide who will lead the performance;
- think about who will make up the supporting cast;
- consider what control you will have over the stage or setting;
- know what props you will use to support your performance;
- think about how you will pre-sell the event;
- decide how you'll know whether it has worked.

Define the event

First, define the event. Although in this section we talk about the importance of managing impressions up to the event itself, it is nonetheless vital that you are clear what the event is – when it starts, how long it will run and when it will be considered by the participants to be over. For example, you may be preparing a series of questions you have been asked to deal with at an important committee meeting. What you say to key committee members in advance of the event will be formative in terms of how they perceive your performance but it will be how you handle the questions themselves at the committee meeting that will make the difference. For the purposes of the exercise the event will begin before the 'event' actually begins.

Of course, it doesn't mean that you necessarily share your understanding of the start and end points of the event with the audience. It can be precisely because of the way that you manage the aside remarks and segments of communication beyond those points, where the event is deemed to be over, that you can achieve the outcome you want. For example, it's easy to assume that when a job interview is over and you are relaxing with the panel chairperson on the way out of the interview room that it is OK to sigh with relief and make unguarded remarks. However, other panel members may be extremely interested in what you had to say during those moments. The television detective *Columbo* made those 'there's just one more thing' questions his hallmark and showed, albeit in fiction, that people will give all manner of detail away in unguarded comments.

It is vital that you are clear in your own mind when an event begins and ends. In terms of impression management all segments of the event – from the very start through to the end – are in critical territory. If your audience believe that they are likely to see the real you during those moments when the performance appears to be over, their attention level will increase. It is important to 'turn' this expectation. If people think you are more truly you when you are offguard, then appearing to be offguard but actually keeping to the same message will make a bigger impact. Carefully managed asides or off the records can help you enhance your impact.

Decide on the desired outcomes

Essentially: what are you trying to achieve? When you are defining your desired outcomes you should be realistic. For example, if you are giving a report to a committee, it may be that you would like the committee members to think that you are completely in control of the situation having seen and heard your performance. However, if you are realistic you will probably settle for them not stopping you doing what you have started, for example. You need to be able to make a judgement about how far you can change people's impressions of you in a single meeting. As discussed elsewhere, your impression will be a product of how they have seen you in the past, how others see you and what you do. However, clearly, a sustained campaign of casting yourself in a particular light will have an impact.

If you are preparing for a vital presentation to staff, which will determine whether you are able to progress restructuring plans, you may define the event as all actions you take and conversations you have with anyone connected with the presentation up to and including the event itself. From experience, we know how important the comments made before an event can be in terms of our impression of the event. Think, for example, of the Chancellor's Budget. Each year, there are leaks, comments and speculation before the event. It may be that everyone anticipates tax rises in a Budget. The repetition of that expectation might help prepare the ground from the Government's point of view. In the context of rumours of a 3 per cent increase in taxes, a 1.5 per cent increase will seem palatable. However, without helpful speculation, a 1.5 per cent increase could be interpreted differently. In the process of managing outcomes it will be critical to take account of the pre-sell, sell and post-sell. This means what you say before the event starts, what you say during it and what you say once it has ended.

Define the audience

You need to be clear about the audience. It does not follow that, to use a committee example, only those members who appear at the committee meeting constitute the audience. Certainly, in order that the event is a worthwhile investment, that would be your assumption. However, there may be councillors who would not intend to attend the committee meeting but may still be asked for their views. In terms of your planning, they would be taken account of in the pre-sell – what you say before the event – but such persons would still be defined as audience.

But in any given group it is worth considering how it behaves towards information. Here is not the place for a detailed analysis of group behaviour but think on the way that groups can act. For example, the pack mentality. Imagine you have been asked to present your views on restructuring your unit. You may know that there are a number of councillors who are likely to dislike your approach. Think of the outcome should negative voices set the tone of the meeting early on. Were those voices to gain momentum you could easily find your ideas being rounded upon and quickly dispatched.

Gather all market information

Market information is a critical part of event management. You will need to know as much about your audience as possible. If the event is a job interview, who will be interviewing you? What is their background? It is reasonable to assume that professional background will give you some insight into their outlook. You may be interviewed by a director of education, who may well be a former teacher. Their thinking may be steeped in an educational tradition. They may be much more sensitized to good grammar, proper sentence constructions, inconsistent word meanings and appropriate vocabularies than other professions. If your presentation used split infinitives or in lists failed to mark out separate items by ending the previous one by semicolons, that may significantly shape their impression of you.

Decide what kind of impact you want to create (including the five senses)

Clearly, this will be related to the desired outcome you want. However, if you think through the ways in which we gather impressions it is rare that we rely on information coming from one sense. We are as likely to remember the way that someone looks as much as what they say. We may remember how they smell – many people, men and women, use perfumes to create a particular impression. Even touch becomes a factor when you consider the way that handshakes are interpreted. This could equally be applied to the feel of the paper on which you print your CV and how many times have we lamented the quality of an evening meal because the taste of the coffee fell short of our expectations?

So think through your performance in terms of all five senses. You may not use all but you should at least be conscious that others may use them to reach a view of you. It is a matter of deciding how particular sense management will be interpreted. Some bakeries, for example, pump the smell of fresh bread into their shops and that tends to lead us to buy more bread. We expect those smells when we shop for bread so the impression is consistent. However, if you decided to do a presentation to the full council in an unshaven state, the fact that it is a fashion statement may be lost on some councillors.

Who will lead the performance?

If you are working with others to create a particular impression you should approach the event with the same degree of seriousness as you would any performance. It will be important to know who will say what, where and when. Imagine you were putting together a presentation to a committee on proposals for working in partnership with a private sector company. If you, as an officer, were making recommendations to the council you would need to think about how you should position yourself in relation to private sector partners. You might, for example, simply set out the criteria against which any partnership should be judged. You might then stand back and allow others to make their presentations (perhaps the partner organization) before coming forward again to put together the main findings and recommendations.

Earlier we talked about press conferences. These are no less important as events. Imagine you were briefing the press on issues facing your authority. You would be mindful of the way in which officers and members, particularly where you are sitting at the same table, could be seen. It is highly unlikely that an officer would chair a press conference where a councillor was at the table except for very specific reasons. It would send out the wrong signals to the audience about who actually ran the authority.

Who will be the supporting cast?

If you are trying to sustain a performance of any kind you will need to make judgements about who might help you do so. If you were making a presentation to committee on changes to a health and safety policy the presence of a health and safety expert could well help but with all communication you will always have to be conscious of attention and focus. The longer you talk the less attention you will get – attention wanes over time and the more characters you add to an event the more your audience could focus on. It may be that in focusing on 'off-screen' people they will miss your essential message. Equally, it may be that you want to create that kind of diversion in order to take attention away from what you are saying. It depends largely on what you are trying to achieve and on your judgement about who will help you do so.

What control will you have over the stage or setting?

The location for any event adds meaning to it. If that location is in your control you will be in the best position to determine what kind of meaning you wish to add. For example, you may be hosting a briefing session for members in a committee room. If you arrive early you could change the way that the room is laid out. Think for a moment on the difference that simply changing the seating can make. If chairs are in rows all facing towards the front then you will limit opportunities for discussion (people find it difficult to make eye contact) and focus attention on the person at the front. If chairs are in a circle you will maximize the opportunity for interaction but you may find it more difficult to gain attention.

If you are not in control of the setting – as you rarely are in a job interview – what can you do to exert control or influence? When you go into a room to be interviewed you may not be able to change anything but by focusing attention on yourself by means of a presentation you may be able to change the way that others see you. Knowing the degree of control you will have over the setting will be an important factor in judging whether you are able to achieve what you want in a particular event. Once you have established that, you will need to decide what effect changes, in the setting will have on the meaning of what you are trying to do.

What props will you use to support your performance?

When we get married there are a number of props that help others to believe that the event is real. A wedding dress is an important part. The food we eat and wine we drink are determined, to a large extent, by convention. If we use those conventions then we will recreate a wedding in our audiences' minds and, while the props will be different in our interactions in a council setting, the principle is of equal importance.

Take business partnerships, for example. Certain conventions are prevalent in such relationships. Businesspeople will expect business cards, introductory and follow-up letters, meetings in places where business is conducted and so on. To some mobile phones are an essential business tool but it is worth bearing in mind that the meaning of whatever props you choose to use should be considered in terms of the audience with whom you are communicating.

How will you pre-sell the event?

If you are going to go to the trouble of setting up an event you will need to make sure that your target audience is there. Do they know about it? What plans do you have to make it in their interests to be there? This is important so far as the individual is concerned but the stakes may go up considerably if you have involved many others in the performance. Imagine you have arranged a press conference, for example, to allow your authority to explain what it is doing on 'best value'. It might be an ill-judged thing to do since it would be unlikely to gain much media attention but such things are done. Now, if none of the media turn up (as can easily be the case) others will feel exposed. Your own credibility may suffer and in terms of your overall strategy you may take several steps backwards.

Like all events, those who need to be there need to know that they are invited. Your job as the event organizer is to make sure that they get there.

How will you know whether it has worked?

In the end, it is difficult to get reliable information about how you are really seen but it will be important to keep that under review. When you put together your strategy one of the tasks was to consider how others saw you. Repeating that exercise on a regular basis would be useful. This is not such an odd thing to do since it forms a major part of most personal appraisal processes. When you are appraised your manager should tell you clearly how they see you. If you are engaged in an appraisal system, which gives your staff an opportunity to say what they think about you, then this will provide you with useful and usable information.

However, in improving your brand, since your position is as much a product of what you do, you alone will know whether you are doing the things which will make a difference there. If you are seen to be a remote manager who is not close to staff, simply saying you are will make no difference at all. The Americans say 'walk the talk' and that's what you'll need to do, but moreover, if you are perceived to be a short-term player – one who is doing this for just a few weeks – then ultimately that is how you will be seen.

We all know how vacuous others appear to be when their words are not followed by actions. Those with weak reputations are often those who leave behind them a trail of unfulfilled promises. Others who deliver, and often those who ask nothing for it, will be remembered as such. However, where you wish to ensure that you, your staff or your council are recognized for the work that has been done, you might want to consider how you manage information about your performance as well as the performance itself.

3 The importance of communication with staff – winning hearts and changing minds

We would all like it if the people who worked for us were happy all of the time. That way they would go out and talk positively about working for us. In the ideal world, every member of staff would be told about things that were happening by their manager before they read it in the local paper. They would believe the memos and newsletters that they were sent – they wouldn't distrust them as some form of internal propaganda and they would feel free to talk about their views on how to move things forward. Honesty would be the hallmark of communication.

That's a laudable ambition and worth working towards. In the meantime, it's important to recognize that talking and listening to staff is a critical part of winning their support, and as for earning their trust, that is central. However, you will need to build slowly and hard to do that. You will also need to recognize that trust is easily lost and once it goes it's difficult to get it back again.

In this chapter I will focus on internal communication. I will suggest that the most important purpose for internal communication should be to win staff over to the council's vision. Based on thinking developed by MORI, I will examine ways in which staff can be helped to feel so committed to their authority that they will become advocates and actively 'talk the council up'. I then look at ways in which the thinking of Chinese strategist Sun Tzu might help authorities to define the purpose of their internal communication.

Next I will consider a couple of exercises that might help staff in understanding and interpreting the mission for their authority, which should be at the root of communication. Finally, I will consider some of the barriers that may prevent effective communication.

WINNING STAFF OVER TO THE COUNCIL'S VISION

If there is a body of people who know what your authority is like, warts and all, it is the people who work for you. So, where you might produce a cynical reaction in the minds of those who only discover that your response on planning applications is not what it's cracked up to be only when they apply for one, there is not much you will be able to hide from your own people. Users use your services only occasionally, your staff are there all the time and, yet, the techniques that are often used internally fail to take account of this.

Councils are full of feel-good newsletters which bear no more resemblance to the truth about how it is to work there than *Alice in Wonderland*. Moreover, because there is not a tradition of really listening to what staff say, other than through trade unions (where it is concerned with a different purpose), the fact that you are talking a load of rubbish to your staff is not known and is, therefore, ignored.

It is, therefore, vital that communication with staff is purposeful. It could be argued that the following purposes are important:

- listening to what staff have to say about the organization and its leadership;
- giving staff information they need to be able to do their job;
- giving staff a clear sense of direction;
- giving staff a means by which they can develop a sense of belonging to your authority;
- providing a means of examining difficult issues which affect all staff in an objective way.

It is not that councils do not want to communicate with purpose. The problem is the lack of clarity over purpose. Many authorities have gone a long way towards trying to develop purpose – through the creation of vision and mission statements – but they face the danger of a *reality gap* by neither dealing with what the authority does now nor looking realistically at what it might be able to do in the future. The trends towards Investors in People should not only help local authorities develop clear, measurable corporate and departmental purpose, it should involve staff in defining and delivering that purpose. In many authorities, the places where difficult issues can be addressed with staff – internal newspapers and other forms of internal communication – are usually the last places to look for such things.

Newsletters do, however, focus on visions, but visions, if they are to move people, have to be grounded in a reality that people can touch. If communication is to be about winning the battle for hearts and minds, then those who would lead the charge need to be clear about what flag they are trying to rally staff around. Vague and vacuous statements such as 'serving the public better' tell neither staff nor customers about the authority's mission.

There is also an apparent fear of truth. In many authorities staff are more likely to find out what is going on inside their authority by reading publications published outside. Local media are not afraid of the truth. They are not afraid to talk about internal problems in councils for what they are. They have no fear of pointing out hypocrisy and hype when they see it and for that reason, survey after survey will show that staff will look to their local paper to find out what is going on in their own place of work. This is a shocking fact for communication managers. Staff will buy a local paper to find out what is going on in their organization and reject the free information they are given in staff newsletters.

There are practical difficulties in the time it takes to produce newsletters. With the best will in the world local authorities will always lag behind local papers in managing information. However, it is possible, through the use of e-mail, to send out mass-mailings to staff bringing them up to date on key issues and, although not everyone is on e-mail, it is better to reach 80 per cent of the people you need to talk to and have them believe that at least you are trying than rely on the local rag to put its own spin on events.

There seems to be an assumption on internal newsletters that as long as you show lots of pictures of the leader shaking hands with recipients of 'best suggestion schemes' then staff will feel that everything is fine and we'll all be able to sleep well at night. As long as your internal newsletter ignores the real effects of early retirement, or the problems with performance indicators, or fails to adequately address members' away-days or councillors' allowances, then the people who work for you will look elsewhere for their information.

However, apart from the fact that your staff need to know what is going on for the purpose of doing their job there is another crucial factor. In many towns and cities the local authority is the biggest employer. Potentially, given the number of local government staff which are employed in the United Kingdom, 2.5 million, this part of the public sector should have an excellent press. We all know that is not the case and staff, if they admit to working in local government at all, are as likely to berate their authority as they are to praise it.

APPLYING THE RELATIONSHIP HIERARCHY MODEL

MORI have conducted research into what turns customers into advocates of the places where they shop. They suggest that consumers will go through a number of stages, beginning with awareness, before becoming an advocate for the organization. This is where the consumer is so committed to the organization that they would be prepared to recommend it without being asked.

The central concept to this model is that the key relationships of a business can be thought of in terms of a hierarchy. At the base is Awareness which includes not only what someone knows about a company but also how they know it and the opinions they have of it.

The next level is Trust based on their favourability towards the business overall and their impressions, feelings, beliefs, knowledge and experience with it. This is a precondition for moving up to the next level where the individual enters into some kind of Transaction with the company.

The individual then moves up to the level of Satisfaction which means that their expectations were at least met, and in some cases surpassed. We then believe there are two further important levels. The level of Loyalty or Commitment implies not only a willingness to re-purchase (in the case of a customer) but also to recommend the business to others if asked their advice. The highest level is the level of Advocacy. At this level the individual is so impressed by the business that they will recommend it to others without being asked.

(Peter Hutton, Director, MORI)

When talking to staff it is vital that the activity moves beyond the trite and is purposeful. Staff do not, for example, enjoy spending time being communicated with about communication. There is simply too much work to do. So make sure communication with your staff has a purpose because the time and effort spent on it are resources being used for another end.

REDEFINING INTERNAL COMMUNICATION

Put to one side the simple idea that it's good to talk. Talking in this context has to have a purpose and be a part of a communications strategy. To what extent has your authority examined the core components of turning your staff into advocates for your council? After all, if your staff were able to talk your authority up – at the point of delivery – then that would be one way in which you could move your internal and external image further on.

In this section we look at two approaches towards achieving this aim. In the first we follow the thinking of MORI outlined above. In the second we look at what military strategy might offer internal communication.

TURNING STAFF INTO ADVOCATES

Awareness

How aware are your staff of what your mission is? Do they know why you exist, what you are doing to realize that, and how far you have travelled so far? Are they with you or do they attend in spite of any corporate mission? Are they aligned with their department rather than with the council?

Trust

Trust is a vital part of communication. If people believe that what they are being told has a side or a spin to it, then not only will they spend time looking for that, they will not be fully focused on what you are saying. Do you have some way of measuring how much staff trust your internal communications? Do they read about what is going on inside the council in the local newspaper before they get it from senior management? What actions have you taken in recently memory which might have precipitated a loss in trust?

Transactions

Do the people who work for your council voluntarily enter into transactions on internal communications? Do they seek out newsletters or even memos or are they simply binned? Do you know?

Satisfaction

With all the talk about staff as ambassadors few councils we have visited have ever really attempted to find out whether staff are actually happy about the ways in which they are being communicated with. That's not to say it's not actually going on. Indeed, it should. One of the problems is cost. Regular staff surveys take time and cost money and can promote a culture of introspection when the real business is going on outside the council, but there are two things to wrestle with here. First, what measures would staff use to determine whether they are happy with internal communication? Second, what steps will you take to achieve that degree of happiness over a longer period of time?

Loyalty

Do you have the loyalty of your staff? Are they happy to talk about working for you when they are in the community? What about staff turnover – how does it compare with other local authorities? Do staff feel that they have a stake in what you are trying to achieve? Remember, that in these days of consulting and involving communities, staff may feel that they are more likely to have a voice when they're not in the building.

Advocacy

MORI's 'Excellence Model' makes it clear that there is a strong relationship between employee satisfaction and their commitment to a company's success as well as their commitment to quality and being an advocate for their organization and what it does.

> Some 41% of those who are 'very satisfied' with their jobs will 'recommend their employer's products or services without being asked', this declines to just 4% of those dissatisfied with their job. Indeed, a third of those dissatisfied with their job will actually 'talk unfavourably about the employer's products or services without being asked'. In other words they are negative advocates actively taking value out of the business.
>
> (Peter Hutton, Director, MORI)

What do you know about the way that your employees will feel about your services when they're out there? Do your bin-men talk their service down? Do staff moan to members of the public?

These are difficult questions. In each area they would need to be handled sensitively. In the end, it can be very tricky to gather information on these issues without raising suspicion. Perhaps, first you need to make it absolutely clear which way your council is going and stick to that path. One way of looking at the council mission is through the eyes of military strategy. It is to this area that we now turn.

AN ARMY ON THE MOVE

Think of your authority as if it were an army working towards a common aim. Each department would be a division with its own tasks but they should be a part of a wider task. The leadership, whether it is through an executive board, or through the council, would exercise its control through its senior officers. Like all effective armies it would need to have a clear plan, clear rules for action and clear sanctions for those who do not comply.

As the changes in military organizations over the last 150 years show, the nature of these rules and relationships within armies have changed immediately. Up until the 1870s all except the officers were assumed to be illiterate and, therefore, needed to be in view of those who could follow orders. The German army that invaded France in the 1870s was the first to extensively use maps. This changed the rules and relationships of communication, but they were still there. These changes continued through to the 1870s and 1880s where groups of soldiers in guerrilla armies of special units were given orders over which they had a considerable degree of autonomy. In all armies there are sets of relationships, but they do not have to be simply command and control ones.

The purpose of those in charge would be to identify need and take action to achieve that need within the framework. That action may mean deploying your own staff where you have the resources. Where you had no resources, nor the responsibility, but wanted to satisfy the need you could develop partnerships. Internal communication should be purpose-driven. It must ensure that everyone knows their job within the context of the overall mission. It must mean that everyone could have all of the information that they would need to carry out that job. It must also mean that conflict that arose is dealt with so that any dissent from the common mission was resolved. The military analogy can be useful. Where the military situation exists and a member of an army sets out on a mission but does not know what that mission is, there is a potential disaster.

But do we all share a common mission in local government? It would mean that each job was in some way contributing towards that mission. It would also mean ownership of the mission.

In *The Art of War* the Chinese philosopher Sun Tzu stated that in order that an army might win it must take account of five factors. His work might offer some insight when you consider that winning the hearts and minds of staff can often seem to be a battle.

The way

According to Sun Tzu, 'the way means inducing people to have the same aim as the leadership, so that they will share death and share life, without fear or danger'. Clearly, in local government there are very few occasions when work is a matter of personal life or death. However, there may be many times when our actions could lead to irreparable damage or great opportunity to our reputation or to image of the authority.

Key questions

How confident are you that in your own section your management goals are shared by everyone irrespective of position?

Could the same be said of the senior management of your authority?

How many chief officers treat their department as if it were a separate entity to the local authority?

How many see their work as being a part of the greater goals?

In management terms 'the way' means getting the staff of an organization or a department to share a common mission. In local government terms this is about vision, about knowing where you are going and about being clear what it will mean when you get there. Critically, it is also about sharing ownership of that goal and the risks associated with failing to achieve it.

In the next section we look at ways in which managers and staff can define and own a common mission.

The season

This is derived from Sun Tzu's *the weather*. In military terms, particularly in ancient China, the time of the year that you fought a battle could have a significant impact on the outcome. Clearly, if the rain was pelting down and your foot-soldiers were trudging through mud then the chances of success could be reduced. Unless, that is, you were the defending army when your chances of success would be improved, especially if your opponent paid no heed to the weather.

In local government terms the season means the political time of the year. Timing is all. If you are proposing a massive change in the direction of your part of the council and to do so you need the support of key politicians then the time when you ask for that is important. You might find the support of the leader less forthcoming in the run-up to a leadership challenge. The national political scene will also have an impact. Few councils with a political party in control will want to be seen to be out on a limb and a potential source of embarrassment as a General Election approaches.

Key questions

What timing factors affect the way that you communicate with staff?

Do staff view your communication during time-sensitive periods with cynicism?

The terrain

Sun Tzu's use of the terrain refers to distance, ease of travel, the dimensions of the territory and the detailed nature of the terrain (is it hilly, marshy, sandy?). In management terms it could refer to the various personnel challenges that lie ahead. For example, when an authority is planning a restructuring, what impact will that have on the quality of service provided to consumers and how will that be dealt with? Also, how long will it take for this internal communication strategy to actually work and take hold? Sun Tzu would recognize that sometimes the terrain called for a very long-term strategy and not just a short battle. Most internal communication strategies are much too short term.

Key questions

Are all of your staff aware of the personnel issues which will impinge on the way you communicate with them?

Does your communication only take place in a crisis?

Are there any factors, such as restructurings and reviews, which will have an impact on the meaning of your communication?

The leadership

Here, Sun Tzu and modern day leadership share common ground. The leadership of an organization should be intelligent, trustworthy, humane and just, courageous and single-minded, but is it clear who is leading? There are potentially a number of leaders in a local authority and perhaps there is at times a lack of clarity about who staff should be following:

- the chief executive;
- the leader;
- your committee chair;
- your own manager.

Key questions

Do all of these leaders share a common mission in your authority?

Do we know what to expect of them – is there a job description which says what they do?

Do staff have a copy of it?

Crucially, if you follow what your immediate manager wants you to do, will that be a part of the wider leadership of the organization or a semi-detached strategy for them?

The discipline

This is about getting everyone to agree rules of behaviour for the organization, which apply equally to all. Some authorities have run into difficulties (for the wrong reasons) over members' allowances, for example. When members are rewarded for the work that they do (rightly) at a time when staff positions are under threat then this can cause problems.

Key questions

Do we expect staff to all adhere to the same rules irrespective of position?

Do we have expectations of our employees in terms of what they will say about the authority outside?

Like an army, should we expect pride in what they do and public ownership of the authority's goals?

If we simply expect adherence and demand it, it will not happen. The ownership of a mission has to be earnt, staff will not believe in something simply because they are told to.

Local government is not an army but its mission should be as clear as those which govern the operation of military organization. There is a stress on local authorities communicating more effectively with its local community. Surely, though, it must first communicate with its staff who, after all, are not only in the community but are a crucial part of it.

In the next section we look at ways in which they can be enabled to understand how they fit into and can shape the authority's overall mission.

BUILDING OWNERSHIP

We have discussed the importance of clarity in knowing what you want to achieve through internal communication. Different purposes will require different solutions. If you are simply passing on information then you may choose bulletin boards as a means of getting the message across. If you are seeking to promote understanding, or to persuade, as you might in relation to Single Status, then you will have to take account of what your audiences know now. You will also need to be aware of the sources of information (and in some cases misinformation) there are. Finally, as mentioned elsewhere, you will need to take account of the time they may have available to receive and digest your information.

You may be seeking to build a common agenda – to get all of your staff standing under the same flag. This section looks at some techniques for getting your staff to see themselves as part of a common mission. This can be useful. You can use the material originated in this exercise to help inform the thinking behind any newsletters you create for your team or your authority.

However, the reality is that you can do little unless you first listen to the people you are seeking to communicate with. It is only by listening that you will know what interests them, what concerns them, what form they like to be communicated in and so on. The next section is about listening, a skill which is under-used in most organizations.

LISTENING

In some parts of local authorities listening is a core skill. We probably all have a lot to learn from those of us who spend their time listening closely to what others say. In this last section we look at some of the techniques which might be used to help managers listen more effectively.

There won't be many people in your organization who think we spend too much time listening. It is an undervalued skill. So far this chapter has been virtually devoted to outward communication. Communication, though, ceases to be that unless there's someone there taking it in, and unless we know that from the feedback they give us.

If every one of the 2.5 million people working in local government spent five minutes more each day listening services would improve straight away. It wouldn't cost a penny more on council tax. It would have little or no impact on staffing structures (at least in the first instance) and it would make everyone feel better – if you're being listened to properly then you are likely to feel that your concerns are at least being heard. Moreover, it's achievable.

M. Scott Peck, in *The Road Less Travelled*, says that listening should exhaust us. So intense is effective listening that we need to devote all of our energies to doing it well. Its intensity is such, says Peck, that it is akin to loving someone. And yet, if most of us were to list the key attributes in most jobs, save the so-called caring professions, being a good listener would rarely make it into the top ten.

The drive to listen is not just about good manners. That goes without saying. Listening is also good for the way you conduct business. The reasons are straightforward and yet often ignored.

It tells you whether people have received your message in the first place. It tells you what they think of what you are saying – we rarely listen with our ears alone. It tells you how they want to be communicated with. This last point is what we now want to focus on. If you are devising an internal communication strategy you need to know this kind of market information. Listening will tell you a number of things as the following exercise shows.

 Exercise – listen with intent

Using the following list of questions as a prompt, conduct some field research on different people in your organization. Focus on two or three people and listen to them carefully in different places. You are trying to build up a picture of them in sounds. Try to get as much detail as you can. You will need to listen to them in different contexts – we all change our vocabulary depending on who we are talking to and where we are talking. Try to cross-reference what they say in terms of listeners' different status.

What words do they like to use?

This point has been dealt with in the chapter on personal positioning. Think about the origin of their vocabulary – is it professionally based? Can you recognize a social worker when you hear one? Do they tend to use longer words in front of higher-ranking staff?

How do they use them?

What words do they open their speech opportunities with? Do they ease into what they've got to say in a self-effacing manner such as in the following: 'I wonder if I might make one or two points which others might find helpful'. Or are they bolder? ('There are two points I think we've missed and they are these.') What about the speed at which they speak? Is it fast or slow – broadcasting speed is 180 words a minute. Do they vary the speed, or the tone, or the emphases in their sentences?

How do they structure their sentences?

Do they use complex sentence structures? ('That we are looking at this question in this way leads me to conclude three things.') Are the sentences short and punchy? Do they finish sentences or are theirs full of asides?

How do they manage silence?

Do they leave big gaps between words? That can be one way of asserting power over others. Leaving gaps, with the intention of speaking, can invite others in to fill the void and allow the speaker to say they weren't finished. Also, if others tolerate your silences it can give the impression of either having something interesting to say or it can signal power or respect.

What utterances do they use to fill out the spaces between words?

We all punctuate our speech with little fillers – 'hmms', 'you knows' and the like. What do they use? Are they consistent? Are they always there irrespective of the audience? What tone of voice do they use?

What subject matter do they feel comfortable with?

Do they appear to have one pet subject on which they will always have a view? How do they handle the discomfort of dealing with unfamiliar areas? Do they apply set phrases to smooth over the cracks?

Now that you have all of this information, the next exercise is about putting it to use. There are limitations on the way that this level of receiver detail can be used in mass communication but it can be very powerful on a one-to-one level.

Of all the areas of communication, changing the way we behave inside organizations is the most difficult. None of the issues raised in the last two chapters will be easy to deal with and yet in terms of addressing the future agenda of local government they will be among the most important.

There is change afoot in the public sector. While change may bring opportunity, it also brings insecurity and in the waves of instability people need the reassuring ballast of information. A commitment to be good at talking and better at listening to staff and communities will stand local government in good stead for the next few years. Communicating with staff must involve all the managers in a local authority and not just those with communications in their title. Managing the new local government will require both you and your staff knowing precisely what is going on in the whole local authority, as well as making sure that the whole organization knows what is going on in your part of it. In a world full of change open, honest two-way communication is one of the few ways of diminishing insecurity.

Listening is a good way to move an organization forward. Building a future is another matter. Now, you could ask your staff, 'What kind of future do you think this organization will have?' That might produce a set of useful and usable responses. The next exercise tries to take out some of the predictability that may come about as a result of that question.

STRATEGIC VISUALIZATION

This exercise is about getting your staff (and yourself) to articulate the kind of organization they want to belong to and to use that material to inform a better, consensus-based view of your mission. It works effectively at a team level but can be used across the authority (in small groups). It uses fiction-writing as a way of getting people to think about the kind of authority they want to be part of. By getting people to write about their job in a fictitious capacity you will hopefully gain some insight into what they really think about the future they want to be part of. It is an attempt to get behind the trite words and phrases we all trot out when asked about our work.

 ## Exercise – make my day

Part one – the appraisal

Imagine it is 9.15 am on 5 July 2000. You have just arrived in your office or place of work but you are a client. Write out what it looks like, what the staff are like and what three things they could do so that when you left you were able to think to yourself, 'That really made my day'. Try to write it in free speech, as you might say it. Use no more than 250 words but no less than 200. For example:

The office was quiet. Strange, since at this time of the day these places are normally pretty busy. It wasn't hard to get attention. Straightaway they typed my name into the computer and they were able to take up where we left off on the phone. I explained that I had wanted to come in because I wasn't quite clear about how my planning application was going to work. She wasn't worried. 'People often come in,' she said, 'it's their way of reassuring themselves. It can be awfully complicated'.

We went through the forms, always more complex than they need to be. I mean how many times should you need to give your name? Four separate times I counted. Maria, that was her name, agreed. 'We are looking at ways of making things less complicated,' she said. Then she sighed. 'We've been saying that for years. Nothing ever comes of it but we live in hope' and then she sighed again.

It didn't take long at all for her to explain the whole thing. By the time we'd finished the office was getting busier. A couple came in with young children. Their kids sat and played at the computer and then an asthmatic man came in. Maria's colleague had met him at the bottom of the stairs. Just as he came up to the counter we finished up. Maria smiled at me and then turned to the man and he smiled, too.

You might then isolate three things that made your day:

1. a member of staff who understood your needs;
2. a member of staff looking out for the needs of vulnerable people;
3. a waiting room geared to meet the needs of families with children.

Part two – assembling data

Once each person has completed the first part of the exercise and teased out the key elements, you can then compile those into a separate list and try to pull out common themes or values.

You might isolate things like caring organization, people who look out for each other and so on. Critically, the exercise should tell you about their own vision for the organization.

Part three – synthesis

Your staff will now have given you their views on the kind of organization that they want to belong to. In part three you pull together the key values and the behaviours which illustrate those values and you develop your practices around those behaviours. So rather than saying, 'We answer all phone calls within three rings', which tells you nothing about what you say when you pick up the phone, you will be able to say, 'We *listen* when people call'. However, the latter will only be applicable if it has arisen out of the exercise. In other words, staff will own it because they have isolated this as an essential behaviour.

What this exercise should give you is a non-threatening insight into the kind of organization your staff say they would want to be a part of. It is by knowing such things that you, as managers, will be better able to meet their needs. One of the problems faced by those who carry out communication surveys is that of raising expectations beyond the point where they can be delivered in a reasonable time-scale. And, of course, each time you raise expectations and fail to deliver (it may simply not be feasible) you get one more unfulfilled promise on your tail.

Here is another exercise which might achieve similar results in defining your goals.

 Exercise – the pebble

Another way of getting staff to share a common agenda is to reduce your work to one essential concept. The exercise works well when you ask what is it we essentially do? It means ruthlessly boiling your work down to one thing. That might be challenging but it's not something you need to do alone. You could make it a team exercise. It's better to avoid jargon and make it something tangible.

For example, you might be engaged in working closely with people in bringing about positive changes in their lives, such as in social services. You could say, for example, that you and your staff are essentially pebbles. The pebble is a metaphor because when you drop it into a pool (symbolizing your interaction with clients) the ripples can be felt far from the original point.

Dropping pebbles

If you and your staff can share the metaphor and recognize in it what they essentially do, the next stage is to look for evidence. Working in small groups or pairs identify instances when you have dropped pebbles into people's lives. You might talk of them in terms of the frequency with which you do this or the size of the waves caused. You could extend the metaphor to talk about issues such as multiple interventions when, for example, social services may be dropping pebbles at the same time as education professionals.

The exercise is a way of considering what you do, how you do it and the common mission, in a non-threatening, jargon-free environment. It is on the basis of such an approach that you may be able to consider ways of better sharing information and communicating with each other in order to do your work more effectively.

Obstacles to effective communication

Having and knowing the purpose of internal communication will help an authority bind itself to a clear mission (as will clear and rigorous business or service plans). However, it is important that such thinking is located in the real world and in that context no matter what you want to do there will be forces ranged against you. If there is a battle for hearts and minds it's vital to know who else is on the field. Trying to persuade the staff of an organization to believe in what the organization does is a difficult task because every staff member has the experience of this and other organizations in their hearts and minds already. At the least it makes them cynical, at the most it makes them strongly dislike organizations that have any expectations of their allegiance at all. It is only when you know the enemy that you can deal with it. There are a number of potential enemies to progress.

Habit

This takes the form of existing expectations. If you are to change the way you communicate there may be reluctance simply because it has never been done that way. Inadequate though existing communication systems may be, they at least will be familiar. When you put in a place new measures you will need to identify which habits will need to be broken.

- What do you know of existing means of communication?
- What sources of communication do officers and members find the most reliable?
- How important a source of information is the local paper?

Vested interests

In any status quo there will be winners and losers. When you change the way you communicate some will benefit, others will lose. Identify where losers have vested interests and deal with that in advance of putting your plans in place. For example, internal communication may be managed by the personnel function who may believe that since they are concerned with industrial relations that is where internal communication should take place.

This may mean that internal communications become no more than industrial relations by another means. Consequently, reaching the staff will depend entirely upon the methods of communicating that the trade unions have and may exclude all staff who are not members. If your personnel function has a strong chief officer or a member then they will need to be won over before putting in place any new arrangements.

- What other vested interests are there in your authority?
- Who are the beneficiaries from the current state of internal communication?
- Which important issues do not get discussed?
- Who manages discussion around important issues?

Inertia

This can be a reason for a lack of progress, inasmuch as it takes time to change, or it can be a means of preventing change. Again, it is worth identifying what type of inertia you are likely to encounter, and to deal with it in advance. Clear dates for new arrangements, clear responsibilities for lead officers and proper accountability will ensure that inertia doesn't stand in the way. It is also useful to have clear, very early examples of how successful the communications strategy has been and what it has achieved.

- Where you have developed an internal communications strategy, what landmarks have you set out against which you can measure success?
- What outcomes are you aiming to achieve?
- What are the main inertia barriers to changing the way that people communicate in your council?

Counter interests

This is another matter. Whereas vested interests will be part of the inertia which will prevent progress, counter-interests will be actively working against you. In a complex organization, such as a local authority, it is inevitable that there will be counter-interests with very different goals. These may be more difficult to deal with as they may appear to support what you are doing but in reality are working behind the scenes to destroy the project.

- Is there any evidence of counter-interests working against your authority's mission?
- What communication techniques might they be using to progress their aims?
- Is there evidence of important information being leaked in a way which damages the way it might be received by staff?

Trade unions

This is one very specific vested interest which needs to be taken account of. You may be developing a council-wide publication which may deal with staffing matters. Your vision will need to take account of the legitimate interests of the trade unions who will be seeking to protect and promote the wishes and rights of their members.

- What arrangements do you have in place to ensure that trade union representatives are involved in contributing to the council's communication?
- What arrangements do trade unions already have in place to communicate with their members?
- On what issues are trade unions and the authority at one?
- And on which are they not?

Political dimension

Whatever form of internal communication you use must take account of the political dimension. What will members be tolerant of? How, for example, would they feel about a newsletter which asked uncomfortable questions about their role in the organization?

Whatever form of internal communication you use it must, if it is to be successful, take account of other internal pressures and potential obstacles.

Trading in credibility

In an earlier chapter we talked about the need to be conscious of your credibility if you are to be believed. The same thinking may be applied to internal publications. Like all publications their believability will depend upon a number of factors:

- who the authors are;
- who the publishers are;
- the purpose of the communication.

Most internal publications will begin with zero credibility. If they are going to earn points they must do so consciously. All too often, authorities are reluctant to allow this to happen. Internal publications, after all, need to earn their stripes in the same ways as external media. Most people believe the likes of *Today* on Radio 4 partly because it airs letters critical of the programme and partly because there is no straightforward line that emerges. It does not appear to have an agenda. If it did people would turn off. Every time the programme deals openly with the criticism levelled at it by detractors, or gives the Radio 4 controller a hard time, our respect for it will grow.

As obvious as that may seem, few internal council newspapers will take the same approach. How many would dare ask what the leader does for his or her money. How often do you see editorials on members' attendance allowances, or management harassment at work, or the problems with politically correct language? Rarely. Credibility and the perception of truthfulness comes from getting people to believe that you are pursuing it. Staff will only believe you are pursuing it if they can see it in their paper and recognize it in their work life.

Local government staff are not stupid and staff who work in an organization that they experience as unhappy would have to be very stupid indeed to believe a newsletter that told them that the organization was happy. Never forget that the staff you are communicating with actually work there and are likely to know a lot about what you are telling them. Those who dedicate their lives to public service ought to be rewarded with internal magazines and newsletters which takes them seriously.

If internal communication is to be meaningful it must deal with problems. This book demonstrates that there are some massive challenges ahead. The definition of 'best value' for the individual who works in an authority will not be easy. Moving from a producer-led culture to a consumer-led culture will be very hard. Getting the whole staff to believe that a blame-free authority can become a reality will be challenging. Not everyone will want to take these issues on board. There will be those who will simply sit it out until retirement. Others will say that their authority 'dealt with' compulsory competitive tendering. Best Value won't be any different. Internal communication, whether at the level of the team or of the authority, will need to wrestle with these issues.

In the next chapter we focus on some of the techniques that may be used to talk to and listen to staff in your authority.

4 Communicating with staff – the tools of the trade

This chapter focuses on some of the techniques which may be used to communicate with staff. It will begin by looking at internal publications followed by an examination of team briefings. It will examine the need for all forms of internal communication to be developed through managing credibility as mentioned in an earlier chapter. Essentially, communication, it will be argued, is a costly business and must be justified in terms of achieving specific business objectives. There is a short case study to illustrate this point followed by an examination of other forms of communication, such as gossip, and how they may be used. Finally, the chapter looks at whether authorities should create a communication charter.

NEWSLETTERS AND MAGAZINES

Part of the reason for carrying out the visualization exercise in the previous chapter was to establish what your staff value. Unlike newspapers and magazines in mainstream life, internal publications cannot take the same things for granted. If your publication is going to be purpose-driven it has to be a blend of what is expedient in management terms as well as meeting staff needs. In short, whereas the mainstream media can rely on a diet of sex, crime and disaster this could never be appropriate for internal consumption.

However, because of the way that internal publications are approached – grins and gripes in abundance – this is rarely an issue. If people believe that it will never be any better than glossy propaganda or puff, then a major opportunity to use internal communication as a business tool will be lost, but it needn't be so. By showing staff that the publication will be rooted in their values then you are more likely to engage them. If you include staff values and concerns into the aims and objectives of the publication you will begin the crucial process of winning support and gaining ownership.

As you plan any internal communication, you will still need to deal with a possible mismatch of expectations – senior management wanting something strategic and junior members of staff showing little interest with big picture thinking.

Here are some of the key elements which you will need to take into account as you assemble your publication.

Editorial control

It is important to determine who is responsible for deciding the overall balance of articles. The editor will determine what goes where and how long the article should be but the position of editor of an internal magazine is incredibly demanding. It is either very easy to offend people (probably because you are asking the right questions) or easy for readers to ignore what you produce (because you are not asking the right questions). It is essential from the start to be clear who the editor is and what control he or she will have. Do they, for example, have to check copy with the chief executive? If not what would happen if they wrote something that was problematic?

The editor ought to be someone with news judgement and who understands how to use that judgement to engage readers with the issues that matter. They will need to be sensitive to the needs of various power groups – other officers, key councillors and opinion-formers.

Editorial board

One way of involving people on a regular basis is to set up an editorial board. In the case of a council-wide publication this could mean representatives from each department. This can be useful in gaining support from departments. The danger is that each representative believes that their first loyalty is to the department. This can easily be reflected in the publication, which may look like a rag-bag of the things the directors want to see, and worse, when you look at what those things are and why they're there. Pictures of chairpersons shaking hands can make politicians feel good but do little for magazine interest.

Editorial values

The editorial team should try to be united on their views of the publication – what gets in, why and what doesn't. It should sit within the context of a vision. Crucially, the publication must have a purpose. If it is felt by members of the production staff to be filling in space then it will appear that way to readers.

Vision

This is how the magazine fits into the strategic thinking of the organization, or the department. In what way would this element of internal communication help to achieve business objectives? How would that be measured?

House style

This is 'our preferred way of presentation'. If the publication is to appear to be professional it needs to take a professional approach. We, as consumers, expect consistency in terms of approach, grammar, capitals, etc. Your publication should adopt the same approach. Write down what your policy is and stick to it.

Positioning

Where does your publication sit on the paper stand? Is it a tabloid, broadsheet or magazine? The answer to these questions depends as much on what your readers normally read as it does on your own aspirations. If your staff usually read tabloid newspapers you might find that a tabloid style newsletter gets read. If you want to use a tabloid format you must be able to write simply, with large headlines, decent pictures and a wide range of visuals. It's not that you cannot do the same thing with broadsheets, you can, but expectations will mitigate against that. We have learnt to associate one set of rules with tabloids and another with broadsheets. If you want your publication to be accepted quickly, don't break the mould.

Expectations

Once you begin producing a new publication you will generate expectations. You may say it is a monthly, for example. If so, make it so – don't abandon that after two months and opt for every six weeks. Reliability will be one of the factors which determine credibility. If your resources won't stand up to regular production call it an occasional publication. What you really want is people to look forward to its publication with a hope that it will tell them something. If you get to that position it is criminal to disappoint.

Credibility accumulation strategy

This is the most important and least debated factor of all. You are presumably producing a publication because you want people to read, believe and trust in it. You will, therefore, need to identify what you must do in order to win that trust. You cannot simply assert it. It must be earnt. There are ways in which this can be done as shown in the next section.

Printing non-mainstream or uncomfortable views

Your readers will expect there to be pictures of the chief executive, news on the 'Best Value' front and the like. That's what the management line would be, but if you want to engage people you need to persuade them that this is not simply *management by another means*. You could run articles by people who think that 'Best Value' is a waste of time. Hackney's *'talkback'* has an anonymous letters' page where people can say what they like with impunity. As a result of the success of this page they have a healthy flow of non-mainstream views and the publication has grown in stature among its readers.

Tackling controversial issues

You should deal with difficult issues. Problem pages are amongst the most read in the mainstream media. How serious is sexual harassment in your authority? The chances are that it is rife, if your council is at all representative of the country. It will be important when dealing with the issue that it is given a full airing. There will be those men and women who have experienced harassment. There will also be people who believe that slightly risqué behaviour is simply one of the features of day-to-day life in any organization which employs men and women.

Challenging the status quo

Staff will have a pretty good idea of who is boss in your authority. Your magazine could well support that person openly – a column by the chief executive would be a common feature. You might, though, choose to focus on the pretenders to the throne – the men (and women) who would be monarch. It would be surprising (and unwise) for any of the potential successors to take a public view on this but it would be possible to gather together views from off the record conversations.

Acquiring credibility

There will probably be a local journalist who will be the thorn in your authority's side. He or she will regularly point out inconsistencies in what you say and do. You can almost guarantee that staff will single out his or her views for special attention – it will confirm their own prejudices. Ask that person to write for your magazine. By acquiring a legitimate and credible outside voice you add credibility to your own publication.

Win support for the bad times

The use of the above techniques may lose you support in key circles. There will be those who think that your magazine or newsletter should be closed down. That will be helpful as it will add credibility – staff will be reassured that your publication is actually printing the truth – but it will cause problems. On the positive side, senior councillors and managers will have access to a vehicle which will be read and believed by your own staff. It will also mean that there is at least a spine running through the whole organization. On the negative side, they won't be in a position to control it. Before you launch this approach to your publication you need to let senior councillors know what it might mean and win their support for the project. If you don't get that support, don't adopt this approach.

What's in it for me?

The people you are writing for will be busy. They won't have the time to read the daily paper. Their in-tray will be bulging with documents, papers from the government and all manner of work that they simply haven't had time to read. Be honest with yourself – what makes you special?

However, although you won't have decent writers, a burgeoning budget or excellent graphic design and printing (unless you're very lucky), you could still get them to read your publication. Virtually every one of us will become interested in something if we can first see what is in it for us. So as you start to put together your publication try to find out what they're really interested in. Will it make their job easier? Will it help them earn more money? Will it entertain them? And so on. If you write about personnel issues address the uncomfortable issues (will I lose my job?) first. That way you've got some chance of getting them to the second paragraph.

The following is a case study which demonstrates the way in which a publication helps meet strategic objectives:

Case study: 'Developing publications to achieve strategic objectives', Local Government Voice magazine, by Michael Baker, Managing Editor of Local Government Voice and the Local Government Association's Corporate Communications Manager

The publication of the 'flagship' Local Government Association's policy magazine was an important strand in the mix of launch events and branding activities for the new organization in April 1997. As well as assisting the LGA to position itself as the premier local government organization, the magazine was seen as having a continuing role in improving communications between the LGA and its member authorities, and other interested parties. In terms of content, the magazine expressly promotes the organization's priorities by stimulating debate about its key policy aims.

The magazine aimed to increase the role and influence of local government in all matters affecting the communities served by its local authority readers by promoting innovation, analysis, debate and dialogue.

As the primary external communications vehicle for a unique new organization, the magazine was able to attract high-calibre writers and columnists, use strong design values, take risks, explore and comment on the changing national agenda in a challenging and often controversial way. This provided a new service for readers not currently available from the traditional trade press.

The mainly feature-based format dealt with policy development and debate, new thinking in British politics, views from opinion-formers in the media, opinion, commentary and analysis. The LGA's bimonthly 'flagship' magazine had a key role in improving communications between the Association and its 500 member authorities in England and Wales and its wider community of interest.

Local government, which spends £76 billion a year providing services to 50 million people, is undergoing immense change in its organization and role, particularly since the May 1997 general election. The magazine has a core function in 'managing' the terrain for debate on those key subject areas affecting change in the sector.

The principal target audience is senior local government politicians and managers in nearly 500 local authorities in England and Wales. The other target audience is an external policy network of ministers, MPs, MEPs, working peers, civil servants, political parties, academics, media commentators and national organizations.

The magazine's quality of production and visual appearance was designed to convey the impression that the LGA was a leading national body, on a par with the TUC and CBI, and should be capable of favourable comparison with news-shelf current affairs and professional magazines. The presentation of the magazine was aimed to demonstrate the same self-confidence, flair and purpose that the LGA was showing as a new unified organization speaking as the national voice of local government and local communities.

It has explicitly aimed high, beyond the normal expectations of a local government audience. The first issue of the magazine in May 1997 was billed as 'A new magazine for a new era' following the formation of the LGA from the merger of three organizations in April 1997 and the Labour Government taking office after the May 1997 General Election.

A communications review carried out by MORI on behalf of the LGA in August 1997 found a 'high awareness' of *Local Government Voice*, particularly among chief executives, although there had only been one issue at the time of the research. Publications were generally seen as well-written, well-produced, authoritative and timely. The review showed the magazine had proved to be useful to the core audience of senior politicians and managers.

The MORI Communications Review (carried out in August 1997) found that:

- Overall ratings for LGA communications are very positive. This relates to a perception of good performance nationally (a finding from qualitative research); communicating with local authorities is seen as a core function of the LGA.
- The LGA is particularly highly rated on its role in promoting a positive image of local government – evidence of a perceived strong performance at the national level.
- Key strengths are seen to be timeliness of the information, its topicality, its relevance and that it is well-written.
- Independent readership research among the leading players in local government carried out after the first six issues appeared suggests that much of that original vision is being realized.

Main findings of the telephone survey conducted by NOP Social and Political in April 1998, based on 200 respondents (100 chief executives and 100 council leaders), showed:

- 83 per cent have read or looked at a copy of the magazine in the last two months.
- 79 per cent say that they read their own copy. 20 per cent say that the copy they read was passed on to them by someone else.
- When asked, two-thirds (66 per cent) say they pass on their copy of the magazine on to someone else once they have read it.
- A half (48 per cent) say they read at least half of the magazine.
- A third (33 per cent) keep their copy for reference purposes.
- Three-quarters (75 per cent) agree that the magazine is of value to them in their work.
- Two-thirds (66 per cent) agree that the LGV is an authoritative magazine.
- The vast majority (82 per cent) agree that LGV is a well-written magazine.
- Over two-thirds agree that LGV provides a forum for debate on local government issues.

We also have pointers to future development. The NOP survey revealed that:

- Over half feel that increasing the number of issues of LGV to make it a monthly magazine would be a positive change.
- Over half say that providing an electronic version of LGV on the World Wide Web so that it is available on the Internet would be a positive change.

The strategic vision for the magazine arose out of a clear understanding of the underpinning messages and values in the corporate identity exercise. My direct involvement in the corporate identity development team was key to developing plans for a range of corporate publications, each with its own particular job to do. It was seen as crucial that the new organization achieved a high standard and strong visual identity in all its publishing output so that the new direction and philosophy of the LGA would be visible to all.

An external design audit of the LGA brand after the first year of the new organization put its value as a £1.2 million asset and confirmed that the brand was increasing in value.

TEAM BRIEFINGS

The problem, of course, with newspapers or magazines is that they are one-way traffic. Short of the occasional letter from 'disgruntled' of 'wherever', it is not a vehicle for finding out what people think, but in a changing culture you need to hear what people have to say. For that reason, although newspapers can help promote the way ahead they can do little more than signpost and pick out the interesting bits.

Team briefings can offer more. An effective team briefing system can cascade important information down a system quickly so that everyone shares the same data within the same time frame. At the same time information and views will be fed back from staff.

How does it work?

The top team in an authority will determine what information must be heard by everyone in the organization and when. They will then shape the core brief – the key facts that they want everyone to know, complete with contextualizing paragraphs (when they need to know now). The rest depends upon the size of the organization and the range of the team briefing but the essence is that people are briefed in teams. The top team will brief the next layer who will in turn each brief their layers and so on until everyone knows what's going on.

The system can be made considerably richer both by building it into existing regular team meetings and by encouraging managers to localize the briefing by building in material that is relevant to their team. In addition, at each level team briefers may have the opportunity to pass information and feedback upwards. Team briefing can be an efficient system for mass information but it can too easily be subject to the same difficulties that newsletters fall foul of.

Fear that confidential information will leak into the local media can mean that virtually nothing controversial will ever appear in a briefing. This will mean, in turn, that if there is anything controversial going on, the last place you would look would be in the team briefing sheet. Further, the expectation of a leak will confirm in the minds of those receiving the information that it is absent because they are not to be trusted. What follows is a realization that the system is symbolically meaningless – it is about being seen to communicate rather than communicating important information and therein lies the problem. As a means of binding the organization to a common purpose its mode of operation achieves the reverse.

THE GOSSIP NETWORK

The fact is that people have an uncanny knack of finding things out. The best kept secrets are no more than *facts in waiting*. Sooner or later most things come out. The gossip network is the route that facts take to spread their way across an organization. So effective are the gossip networks that a juicy fact behaves more like a virus in terms of the speed and mode of transmission. It will adapt to meet the needs of the group who are spreading it around. The result is often distortion and misinformation. However, because information is coloured by the process – we are not supposed to know it, therefore, it becomes interesting – it is one way in which you can get your message across quickly.

If it works use it but first you've got to know how it works. It's not enough to know that if you say something in the corridor outside your office the leader will hear it over coffee 30 minutes later. If you are to use gossip networks as a means of transmitting (and receiving) information you need to know which routes it will take and that means an audit. You need to know, without making it public, who gossips to whom, when, how and why. Once you understand the means and motives of gossips you can then put them to good use. Clearly, this is not something you can carry out detailed questionnaire-based research on. Simply asking the question would blow the strategy out of the water.

Testing the networks

One way of uncovering the transmission lines is, over a period of time, to release information into the network and see where it goes. There are a number of fairly straightforward informal techniques for getting information out into networks without looking as if you mean to.

The photocopier

Leave key papers on the photocopier at a time when you know that certain persons are likely to encounter them. They need not be of a too serious nature but they do need to contain something about them, such as the inclusion of words such as private and confidential.

Overheard remarks

Making remarks in front of others at a level when you have to strain your ears to pick them up can be very effective. 'I shouldn't be telling you this', said to the right person, will at least get your story on its way.

Leaving your office door open, letting people peruse your desk or putting your in-tray in a prominent place are all guaranteed, provided that there is something interesting to look at, and that you don't do it all of the time, to arouse interest. The gossip network will work whether you like it or not. People talk about each other and about things which might affect their lives. At least if you know how it works you might be able to use it at some stage.

Of course, we all know that it's not just the means by which people find out about things which interests them. It's also the spin. If something has a sala- cious side to it that can make it much more interesting. We know, for example, that sex sells but we're not suggesting that you should send round messages about proposed restructurings on the back of a sex scandal in the local corri- dors of power. We're suggesting that when you put information into the net- work, by whatever means, you should think about what is going to get people interested in it.

Learning from gossip

We can all learn a lot from gossip. While some information we pass around our networks is important for the work we do, little of it will excite us. That is not the case with gossip. Simply calling information 'gossip' makes our ears prick up. It is worth thinking about why gossip does interest people to see whether there are lessons we can learn from the point of view of our general communication. Think of the best piece of gossip you have ever heard then ask the following four questions:

1. What did it concern?

Knowing the subject matter will tell us something about the kinds of things we like to hear about but it will also tell us something about those things others are interested in. We will rarely hear gossip 'straight from the horse's mouth'. It will have passed through a few networks before it got to us. So what was it about the subject matter that gained and kept our interest and how might we apply that thinking to other information we want to pass on? Try to think a bit deeper here. While subjects such as the sexual lives of our colleagues might be gossip material there is probably more to it than that. Gossip, for example, about government ministers' private lives is more interesting because they may not be practising what they preach. Gossip in that case is really concerned with hypocrisy.

2. Where did you hear it and did that make it more interesting?

What does location tell you about information? Think about where you heard it and reflect on whether it might have been more or less interesting had it been heard in a different place. What was it about the location which interested you?

3. What about the language?

When you hear gossip, how do you know it as such? It might be that the speaker says, 'Here! Got some juicy goss for you' or it might be something about the way they speak. If so, try to define those qualities. Could they be applied to other forms of communication to make them more interesting?

4. What about the speaker?

What was it about the person who told you this gossip that added weight to what you heard? Was that person a reliable source? Were they known for having their finger on the pulse? Again, try to dig deeper. Understand how the qualities they had made them more interesting. It may be that you will be able to apply that thinking to your own communication. For example, if there was a particular message that you wanted to get round the office, and you didn't want to write it down, you might choose to give it someone who was known for being a reliable source of information. If you wanted to give it a scurrilous feel you might give it to another and so on.

The next section looks at how you can encourage your staff to communicate more effectively. If the general standard of communication goes up, and at the same time it becomes more purposeful, then the organization will benefit.

WRITTEN COMMUNICATION

In any year local government officers will probably write more words than the average best-selling author. Think of what you put on paper or PC this week – letters, memos, e-mails, committee reports and file notes. Local authorities are not verbal organizations – virtually everything is written down and yet how often do officers look closely at how they write? How many authorities train their officers in the art of effective writing? Some but not many. If councils were able to ensure that every piece of written communication met the needs of the audiences at which they were targeted, positive perceptions of local authorities would increase a thousandfold in one week. Too many local government officers believe that the interaction is complete when it leaves their desk. They fail to realize that it is only complete when the person it is sent to understands and acts upon it. The point is not to send the letter but to fully communicate its contents.

The following section is a four-point plan for improving your and your staff's written communication:

1. Get your staff into the right frame of mind

If you are going to have an impact on the way that your staff communicate in writing, you will first have to get them to accept that they can do something about the way they write.

Look at how they got to *here*. If we examine our written communication closely we will quickly recognize its history. Every influence will be there. From the teacher who said, 'You must never begin a sentence with "and" or "but"' through to words and phrases which are the results of professional training (have you noticed how many of your legal staff use the words 'in terms' even when they're not talking business?).

Help them understand the conditions in which they write. When we don't like to write, and most people feel insecure about it, they leave their writing to the last minute. They won't set aside time to think about the audience, the outcomes they want and the time that they will need to make their communication work. They'll do it all in the worst possible circumstances. Effective writing needs the right environment but your staff will also need to be able to consult with others as they put their words together. Is there a culture where people can share ideas and approaches in your organization?

Help them realize that there is always a better way. This is about helping your staff understand and recognize the value of criticism. We can all improve the way we write. However, in order to do so you have got to first accept that there may be a better way of putting things. It's important that you help them understand that this will be painful at first. Many of us approach writing as though it was the deepest expression of the state of our soul – attack it and we suffer. We all need help to be able to improve.

Build a bank of good communication. When your office has begun to improve its written communication, keep the writing that works in a file which everyone has access to. It doesn't follow that what works with one audience at one time will automatically work with another. However, if you are clear about why a letter might have worked in the first place you might be able to import some of the lessons (and the words) as you put together another.

Use your own work as an example. Junior staff may well expect their superiors to pull their work to pieces. In this way 'improvement' can easily get confused with power relationships. If this confusion is allowed to grow it can undermine any attempt you make to help others improve communication. However, if you pull your own work to pieces, and encourage others to help you, particularly junior staff, you will help them appreciate that everything can be done better.

2. Think outcomes

At its worst written communication can be habit-driven. Think of those letters which go out to particular audiences every year at the same time such as those on student grants. We have seen instances where last year's letter is simply photocopied and stuffed in an envelope alongside the cheque. Of course, the same can be achieved on a PC by simply changing the date of last year's letter and sending it out but think about what that says to the recipient. If your communication doesn't take account of your audiences' needs it can fail to engage, or worse it can say to them that you think they matter little and it's not just you, as the author, who is saying that. To the recipient of a letter from your council that's what the local authority thinks. So, again, a systematic approach can help.

What are the audience's needs?

When you write anything think about what the recipient wants, needs and has time for. Picture them in your mind. For example, imagine that you were a teacher at a university and had to write critiques of students' essays. It would be important when writing those one-page summaries to remember that you would not be there to explain your remarks when the student received them. You would have to also remember that the students would have been waiting for their results for a number of weeks, that this work would be important to them, and that individual words, badly chosen, could affect their mood all day. At the same time, you have to remember that they need constructive and honest feedback and all of this has to be achieved within 200 words.

What do you want to achieve?

What is the purpose of what you are writing? Be clear in your own mind first. Is this report about winning support from your colleagues? How do you want your audience to feel when your letter has been read? It might seem strange to even think about feelings but any form of communication will produce a feeling. It's better to be conscious of that and determine in advance which feeling you want – engaged, involved, welcome, etc. Think also of what you want them to do as a result of your communication.

What sort of words and language do your audience use?

Many of us make the mistake of talking to others in language that suits us not those we are communicating with. It's the classic jargon-toting local government officer approach and we're not just talking about acronyms here, which should be banned unless your readers know them as well as you do. It's about recognizing that we tend to assume too much of our audience. It's better to assume nothing and to choose words on the basis of what we know about them. If this seems hard it's because good communication is. But, on the other hand, bad communication is an expensive waste of time and effort. It wastes your staff time but more importantly it infuriates the public and wastes their goodwill. Remember, quite apart from the words you use, not every recipient of your written communication will be as comfortable with language as you are.

How will you get their attention?

We live in an overcommunicated world. When your readers are consuming your work don't forget that thousands of other pieces of communication will be clamouring for their attention. If you are going to have an impact you will need to *think impact*. How will you open your communication? Letters which open 'Re: whatever. Notwithstanding comments made in previous communication' are unlikely to engage a mass audience but somebody will no doubt like it.

How will you know if it has worked?

This is the most difficult part of effective communication but if you are going to communicate for a specific end then you won't ever be effective unless you have some form of feedback. If you are sending out a letter encouraging people to take up a particular benefit, for example, find out how many people did. Encourage your staff to get feedback. Your staff may feel that no feedback means that everything is communicated perfectly, when it probably means everyone who received the letter understood so little that they threw it in the bin. Review your communication regularly and share best practice.

3. Think impact

In any form of communication you will have more attention at the beginning of the exchange than you will as time passes. At the beginning of a letter people read from the top down and from left to right. It's obvious and yet so often forgotten. Reach now into your out-tray and look at a number of documents. Think of them from the point of view of the person receiving them and ask yourself whether you make the most of the attention they will give it at the start.

However, communication is a complex business. Think of a situation in which you feel in control of your communication, at home, for instance. Now imagine that you have to deal with a very sensitive matter. Run the sequence of events in your mind as though you were playing back a video. You might have to say something to your partner which, if not handled well, could cause offence. The chances are that you will not simply come straight out and say it. You will probably ensure that the person is listening to you first. You will need to know that you have their attention, then you may have to give the person some indication of what you want to talk to them about. You might then explain what the problem is, giving them time to take it all in. You will probably want to give them time to think about what you have said and to gain clarification should that prove necessary. Meanwhile the clock is ticking.

It might look like this:

0 seconds – make eye contact

0.5 seconds – smile or nod or acknowledge that you are about to speak

1 – 3 seconds – 'Have you got a minute?' [pause] 'There's something I'd like to talk to you about'.

4 seconds – [pause]

4.5 'I wanted to talk about… ' and so on.

It may be five or six seconds or even longer before you begin to tell the person what you want to talk to them about. You will have judged what kind of impact you want to use in order that the way you approach the communication event supports the message. If you simply rushed at it you might be perceived as insensitive or bullish. You might describe this as low impact.

You might adopt a similar approach in writing. There will be times when you write to people where it is appropriate to break the news gently. This will be successfully executed where you take account of the ways in which your communication will be received.

High impact

There will be times, however, when it will be important to use high impact. If you listen to commercial radio you will hear many examples of high impact communication. Most radio advertisements will be between 20 and 40 seconds. In each of these they will have to engage you, make you feel something about their product and convert that feeling into action – usually they want you to buy the product.

The more quickly you move from engagement to the *call to action* the higher impact your communication will be. Look at the following two examples. The first is a low impact communication. The second uses high impact techniques.

Example one – low impact communication

Dear Mrs Sugget,

You will be aware that you wrote to us on 27 April requesting information about schools which may be available in the area for your children when you move here in August.

I am pleased to be able to pass on the following information which I hope will help you reach an informed choice about a future school for your children.

I can suggest that, given the area in which you have already bought a house, there are three schools – St. Benedicts, St. Martins and St. Peters. I have enclosed the prospectuses from all three schools for you to consider. If you would like further information please call the school concerned directly.

In the meantime, should you require further information please call me on 0900 111 222.

Example two – high impact communication

Dear Mrs Sugget,

Here, as requested, are the names of the three closest schools to your new home. They are St. Benedicts, St. Martins and St. Peters. I enclose their prospectuses. If you would like further information on any of the schools call them direct. If you would like further information from me please call me on 0900 111 222.

Before any form of communication it is important to think about how it will be received and to make a decision on what kind of impact you would like to use in order to achieve your desired outcome.

4. Practice

No one gets anything right first time. But officers will be less prepared to take risks on the real thing unless you are openly prepared to embrace experimentation. So take the approach that all successful industries take – practise first and then do it for real. Set aside staff time dedicated to improving communication. Develop a series of challenging exercises from which you and your staff will learn. Here are some examples:

- Write to parents to tell them that they will not get the school of their choice this year. Aim to reassure them that you have done all you can and intend to make them feel positive about the process.
- Write a brief report to your chair explaining that your unit has not met the challenges he or she has set for you this year. Aim to help them retain confidence in your staff without making excuses or laying blame.
- Write three short letters to a member of staff expressing your concern about the quality of their work. In the first make them feel engaged and enthused. In the second make them feel guilty and in the third make them feel that they are drinking at the last chance saloon.

Keep everyone's writing under review. Don't exempt your own work. If you are able to create a culture which embraces effective communication you will change perceptions of your organization over time.

CREATING A COMMUNICATION CHARTER

In this and the last chapter we talked about the difficulties associated with communication when staff felt that they could not trust what they were being told. This is partly because of a fear of the media finding things out (that you wouldn't want them to find out) and partly through habit we suspect that much internal communication is sanitized. Add to that the idea that communication can be regarded as staff negotiation by another means and that in some authorities parties can be very precious about who talks to staff when. All in all it can be difficult to see how to start to build trust so that your staff can believe they are part of your council rather than simply employed by it.

One way of moving towards honest communication is to develop a *communication charter*. This is about setting out the rules and expectations that an organization should expect of its communication. The starting point for effective communication should be that it is first and foremost a two-way process. There are senders and receivers. When messages are sent they must take account of the needs of the receivers and senders should respond to feedback. A communication charter should be firmly rooted in the real world.

Of course, you can publish all the charters in the world, but getting people, for example, to believe that they won't be blamed when things go wrong (one of the reasons for back-covering memos) is another matter. One way of improving communication is admitting at the outset the reasons why people behave the way they do. Here is a list of behaviours which might apply to your organization. If you find that they apply think about whether you think that they will help or hinder your council.

Knowledge will be associated with power

Staff will hold on to information because they may believe that their owner-ship (and others' exclusion) gives them power over others. It's good to be in the know and a culture which thrives on hierarchies will always encourage ways in which territories can be marked out. Information is one way of setting boundaries.

Control over knowledge is one way in which you can protect your territory

If you are the person whose job it is to maintain the Intranet (but it could be anything) the fact that nobody else knows how to do this could well keep you in a job.

Knowledge is one way of maintaining status

The history of the professions is one of groups of people acquiring and main-taining the boundaries around bodies of information. Only doctors may prac-tise medicine and access to their ranks is carefully controlled.

Powerful people can signal their position by visibly listening less than lower status. Powerful people are busy and don't have the time to listen. They talk, others listen.

Covering your back

If something goes wrong, provided the person above you knows about it – he or she has a copy of a memo explaining your planned actions – you will be OK. The blame will stop with them.

These are, of course, very general ideas. What rules on the management of information apply to your organization? Who gets to see the management team minutes? How widely circulated is your diary sheet? Who gets to go to the ruling group meetings?

The next exercise is about helping you to unearth the various relationships that exist in your council on the basis of who talks to whom. It should help you find ways in which you can use communication more effectively.

Exercise – finding the power lines

Working with people in your unit, and on the basis of existing practice (how they are rather than how you would want them to be), tease out the rules which govern the management of information. Imagine that you are putting together a document as part of an induction pack for a new employee. One clue on this: if you don't feel uncomfortable as you are doing this you are probably not being totally honest. You should be asking questions such as:

■ Who determines who gets to know what and when?
■ What rules do you apply in helping you decide what information to distribute to different audiences?
■ Where does all new information coming into your unit go?
■ Who gets to see it at that point?

Now that you have considered both the way that people manage information as well as the way it is done where you work, you might want to give some thought to developing a communication charter for your council. A charter would simply cover what your employees can expect from managers in terms of information. It would include:

■ staff knowing what priority you, as a manager, place on communication;
■ staff knowing when they can expect to hear things which affect their future or their work;
■ staff being reassured that they will hear important information first from a manager rather than reading about it in the local press or picking it up in the corridor;
■ staff being committed to passing their comments on communication to their manager.

An organization which listens to and talks to itself can be a very powerful thing. It will be one way of making it more effective and efficient. It won't change the world though. It will still be a world where there are redundancies. There will still be those who prey upon each other, in whatever way. There will still be politics and there will still be those who do and those who don't do a good job but where there is a better use of internal communication there will be a better chance of creating a more dynamic, fulfilling and customer-driven organization.

5 Don't mess around with the inevitable – media relations

We begin this chapter by looking at the inevitability of a relationship between an authority and its local media. We examine the case for using the media to the advantage of the council by looking at what benefits can be brought to an authority. We then look at the need for managers to be able to manage their relationship with journalists. Next, we focus on ways in which journalists ask questions before examining a brief survival strategy for handling calls from the media. While this will help managers deal with one-off interviews it will not prepare them for some of the tough and focused interviews they may face. In the latter part of the chapter we look at some of the techniques which may be used to avoid answering questions. Finally, we look at a short case study on the relationship between an authority and the media on a specific story.

The media are often criticized as being the enemy of local government. Whenever you talk to senior officers or members about the local press they will invariably complain that newspapers only print the bad news and permanently omit any comment on all the things that the authority achieves.

Since perceptions to each of us are realities, the press we think we get is the press we get. Even in the face of the objective arguments, which news editors will throw down before us demonstrating the contrary, local government will continue to believe it's hard done by on the media front.

Whether or not the media do give local government a hard time it's worth bearing in mind a number of wider issues about the media that middle managers in local government have to take on board if they are to successfully work with the media. As with every other area of local government, the successful middle manager is active in the pursuit of positive relations with the media and does not just passively accept what happens.

The news media are among the most successful products in the country since they are open to close scrutiny by their consumers on a day-to-day basis. We consume few other products in the same way. News is literally a day-to-day business and on the radio it can be an hour-by-hour affair. What's more, we are able to make instant choices about whether we want to continue consuming it. We can, and do, switch off, when we don't like what we hear. We, as consumers, know the news we want and we choose the products that will give us that.

Each of us will make judgements similar to those made by journalists about the news we consume. Given the multiplicity of news sources, we are in a position to affect news content in a limited way on the basis of whether we consume it or not. If nobody wanted tabloid news, then it would not exist. Newspapers which have failed to meet consumer preferences have gone to the wall. Compared to the slow relationship that any local government services have with the effect of the market choices of consumers on their future, the media have to recognize the rapid impact of consumer choice on their product.

We complain about our own bad news but we're not interested in anyone else's good news. How many of us would really want to tune into the 6 o'clock news if all we ever heard was how good life is? Few of us, if any. Yes, we want good news, but we want it in its place. The '... and finally' slot on television news programmes is probably enough for most of us. So if there's no appetite for good news, then why should we expect it to be written about local government? We know, if we're honest, that we'd far rather read about corruption, fraud and scandal than the fact the 87 per cent of local authorities are able to answer their phones within three rings.

Local managers should start by accepting the inevitability of media coverage. Local government spends £76 billion of public money. It is, therefore, very likely that there will be some strident public accountability, but that's not to say that your authority will always get bad coverage. However, by understanding the things you can change, those you can't and those you can influence, you are much more likely to use the media to suit your own ends.

The media is first and foremost a means of reaching a vast number of people quickly and efficiently but this is often overlooked. Imagine you want to let every household in your town know that you are about to consult them over possible rises in council tax. In a typical area you might be looking at 50 000 households. That is:

■ 50 000 letters or leaflets;
■ 50 000 stamps;
■ the time taken to stuff the envelopes;
■ the time taken to write the letter;
■ the time taken to ensure that everyone who needed to see the letter did;
■ the criticism of spending this much money to ask local people whether you should spend more;
■ the fact that everyone will read the same message but may read it in a different way.

On the other hand you could write the following words on one side of A4 and fax it out to every media outlet in your area:

> Somewhereshire District Council want to know what local people think of a possible rise in council tax of 10 per cent. 'The increase could be used to pay for better services for stakeholders' said the Council Leader, Alf Smith.

However, the media also has a lot to offer local government and, in fact, can help it get closer to the communities it serves.

A MEANS OF GIVING YOUR MESSAGE CREDIBILITY

In Chapter 1 on credibility management we looked at how you are able to accumulate credibility and what factors will determine whether people believe you or not. Whether we like it or not, local people believe the media. They may not believe every word and they may believe one channel more than another. However, that belief is there and it can be put to good use by local government.

It means that when a councillor says something at a committee meeting his or her words will be given extra weight if they are then reproduced in the local media. Information will become more believable depending on the source. Try the following exercise:

 Exercise – examining your own message credibility

A man you have never met or seen before comes up to you in a pub on a Friday night and says that there will be a massive cut in government expenditure on the armed forces within the next year. He then downs his drink and walks out without a further word. There are a number of things that will determine whether you believe him or not:

- Was he drunk?
- Did he look credible?
- Was he well-dressed, clean, was he wearing a military uniform?
- Did he sound credible?
- What kind of accent did he have, was he well-spoken, did he have a speech impediment?
- Why might he have been telling you?
- Was there any apparent motive?
- Did he tell anyone else?
- Were you able to corroborate his conversation, was it reported in the media?

- Did he grin or smile as he told you?
- How old was he?

These factors will affect whether we believe someone or not. Each of us will put a different weight on each of the elements and make up our mind on the basis of the number of ticks someone gets. Think about it for a moment and then imagine the same scene in the following description:

A man in a military uniform, whom you have never seen before, comes up to you in a pub and apologizes for having had a little too much to drink because he's depressed about cuts, which will mean he will lose his job.

For most of us, he will be more believable. It's easier for us to read his motives but the media can side-step a number of personal credibility criteria. It may be that we believe that journalists are in a position to make critical judgements on our behalf. So if the following story appeared on the evening news we might be inclined to believe it:

Informed sources today claimed that the government is planning cuts in armed forces funding.

Now write down what makes a message credible to you.

A MEANS OF MAKING YOUR MESSAGE INTERESTING

Newspapers, radio and television programmes want to make their products interesting. If they fail to do so they will die. At the local elections in May 1998 there was roughly a 10 per cent drop in turnout. The next day local government officers went into work and carried on as before. If they had been working for a local newspaper and the public had showed such a rapid loss of interest, they knew they would be out of a job. So, local media have to work hard to make themselves interesting and if they are not, there is no point in blaming the public the way in which local government does. The media have to be interesting otherwise they go bust. Local government, on the other hand, has the illusion that it can remain boring.

A MEANS OF MAKING YOUR AUTHORITY INTERESTING

Local media take an interest in the activities of local authorities virtually every day. If they were left to promote themselves all the public would see of most stories, which emerge from committee agendas, would be council minutes pinned on notice boards and public notices in small print at the back of local papers. How many authorities would give their information banner headlines, pictures and comment? The fact that the local media do such things (as well as giving endless radio time) can make them interesting.

REACTIVE MEDIA RELATIONS

This next section, focuses on the idea of reactive media relations and offers some initial suggestions for staving off the fear that often appears when journalists call.

The vast majority of media coverage that council officers have to deal with is through reactive media relations. Some authorities manage these relations very carefully, insisting, for example, that press calls go through the public relations office. That can be useful in maintaining an understanding of the kind of coverage the authority is attracting and provides a means of managing the message. However, it can also slow down media relations and potentially encourages journalists to look elsewhere for their information.

In a news-rich area you will need many press officers to handle all of the live stories. The government has such a service through the Central Office of Information (COI) but most local authorities do not have the resource. It's worth remembering that positive media relations can be conducted by anyone who knows their job and who knows how the council want to use the media to achieve their goals.

Partly because of programmes such as Radio 4's *Today*, managers have a fear that the second they answer a call from the local media, they will be subjected to all sorts of cross-examination. Quite simply, that's not worth worrying about. All the same, it can help to have a survival strategy should a journalist call you but first it is important to recognize some of the techniques which journalists can use to find things out.

Most of the journalists that middle managers will deal with will be local reporters and while many may aspire to be the next Jeremy Paxman, few will ever reach those dizzy heights. In the main, they will be driven, as we note in other chapters, by the need to get stories and that is why if you are able to offer them the material they need, on their own terms, they will be grateful, by and large. However, it's worth bearing in mind that all journalists who become media stars began in the local media. Moreover, because of the fashion for confrontational interviews, you could well find yourself in a major inquisition on a minor matter. Forewarned, as always, is forearmed.

Broadly, you will nearly always be quizzed quickly by a journalist working against a deadline. The deadline rules the lives of journalists with a much greater ferocity than the deadline for a committee paper rules local government. Speed of news is always of the essence for reporters and you must come to terms with this requirement. Understand that the pace they have to work at is different from the pace you have to work at. That means that they will have to rely on a number of tried and tested techniques to get information as quickly as they can. Here are a few of them and some suggestions about how you might deal with them. When you read them you may feel that they are all simply clever techniques to get interviewees to say things that they don't really mean, but they are really very clever ways of getting information out of people – quickly. Once you have learnt how they can be used by journalists, you might want to think how middle managers can use them to get their own message across more effectively.

People tell me

This is where a journalist will claim that other people are saying things which you ought to respond to. For example, 'People have said to me that your authority spends far too much time and money on training activities'. This could be the precursor to the question, 'They're right, aren't they?' It's worth bearing in mind that it's more than likely that no one at all will have said anything of the sort. The journalist may have heard a lot of things about training and chosen to conflate them into one question. The problem comes when you answer the question at face value. You might, for example, say, 'Yes, that's a legitimate view'.

That might, however, turn into, 'A senior officer today said that Blankshire District Council spends too much time and money in training'. It is crucial that before any interview you decide what you want to say and then make sure that you only say that. You will also need to be clear about what you definitely don't want to say. If you don't agree with what 'people are saying' you might choose to say, 'Well, they don't say that to me'. Or alternatively, you might enquire who they are but don't expect an answer to that question since journalists don't reveal confidential sources.

Is there not a danger?

This is another way of getting you to admit to the possibility of something. It's a difficult question to deal with because under some circumstances there is always the danger that something will happen. For example, 'Is there not a danger that Blankshire Council will overspend its social services budget this year?' But just because there is the possibility of something there is nothing which says you've got to consider it. The question should, however, be handled carefully. If you say there is a danger then the story could read, 'A senior social services manager today confirmed that social services could overspend its budget this year' and if you deny it (and journalists can build the story from other sources), it could be reported, 'A senior social services manager denied reports that ...'. So, it's probably an idea to be ready to say that you don't think it's useful to answer hypothetical questions.

Do you agree?

Some questions call on you to agree with a particular point of view. You might find, however, that in agreeing with the assumptions in the question this becomes your point of view. For example, 'Would you not agree that in these difficult times less money should be spent at the centre by the local education authority and more should be spent directly by headteachers?' If you agreed to this it could be turned into, 'A local headteacher said today that "less money should be spent at the centre by the local education authority and more should be spent directly by headteachers"'.

Again, if you're sure what you agree with and what you don't you should have little difficulty in dealing with the question. If you're not sure, or if you find yourself being drawn into the question, you might find yourself saying things you will later regret. In this case it may be useful to have a response ready, which makes it clear that this is a complicated issue that needs more investigation before you would agree with anyone who made such a sweeping statement.

Beware flattery

Strangely, flattery does work and journalists can often get to the facts behind a story simply by appealing to our desire to be flattered. If you detect flattery in a business relationship you should understand that it is there for a purpose. It is unlikely, particularly with middle managers, that this technique will be blatant and obvious. It's more likely to be signalled to you through the questioning technique.

For example, 'I can see Hugh (signalling close friendship)/Dr Fraser (signalling respect) the reasoning behind your argument (signalling complexity, alluding to intellectualism) but what I find confusing is the disparity (the "help me because I'm stupid and you're clever" mode) between the amount of money in your budget and the amount you spend on your staff, who are like you, after all, highly thought of (sycophancy)'.

To deal with flattery you must first recognize it is there and be clear about what you *actually want to say*.

Beware the idiot

We are never more likely to take chances in an interview situation than we are when we believe that somehow what we are saying is above the head of the journalist. This attitude is as common among middle managers as it has been the undoing of so many. Basically, if a journalist can get an interviewee to believe that they are an idiot then that might leave the subject exposed. An interviewee can too easily start to believe that the journalist really doesn't have a clue and they may, as a result, start to oversimplify, speak condescendingly and give things away. In short, you are more likely to take chances if you believe that the person on the other end of the phone is somehow not up to it.

So listen out for phrases such as, 'I really don't understand this. I wonder could you explain'. It's almost certain they do understand – and there may be something about the story they understand a lot better than you do.

Anything you (or others) say can and may be used

It's safest to assume that anything you say, from the first point of contact to the last, may be used. It may not be used immediately. An unguarded remark may simply inform the journalist's thinking. For example, a passing comment on the fact that middle managers tend for the most part to ignore the wishes of the chair of the human resources committee may give valuable inside information on the workings of your political management system. Passing remarks, gathered together by journalists from different parts of the newspaper, for example, will start to help build a picture of life behind the scenes.

However, this is one of the most difficult things to control. A journalist may visit a local school, for example. From the minute they walk through the front door to the point where they climb back into the car their eyes and ears will be open. Picture this: the journalist is standing at the school reception waiting to be greeted by the headteacher. They say, 'My goodness, you'd need a degree to understand that mission statement' while looking at the framed text on the wall and the secretary says, 'You're not kidding. They'd be better to concentrate on actions than words'. Ten minutes later the journalist is interviewing the headteacher and says, 'I've spoken to people here about your new management style and they say you're too wordy, all talk and no action. Are they right?'.

However, even if they didn't use that information there they may log in their mind that the secretary could be cultivated to become a source of information, giving away views and perspectives from time to time.

Of course this is difficult to guard against since it is impossible to have a public organization that does not have lots of interaction with the public and, therefore, is exposed to the media. However, as we outlined in Chapter 1, a local authority that knows 'what it is doing', and where all of its staff know what part they are playing, is likely to be one which provides a unified message to the media in all of its interactions.

Stressed out

An interview is an episode. Two individuals will sit together and establish a power relationship. The interviewee will control what facts will be available for consumption. The journalist will control the agenda – they ask the questions. Journalists can too easily assume that the person they are interviewing neither wants nor intends to give them the full story. This is particularly the case on sensitive stories. It's a view reinforced by public bodies' penchant for statements. In an atmosphere of mutual respect and cooperation it will be relatively easy for the interviewee to say what they want, and no more.

However, it's also relatively easy to change the atmosphere within an interview. Journalists can increase the amount of stress that the interviewee experiences by manipulating the cues. We cue each other when we converse, we nod or say 'hmm' to ensure that the other knows we are listening. Think, though, of the impact of not cueing. We all react to the gaping hole of silence in different ways. Some by keeping on talking, others by clamming up. It's also possible to over-cue, to say 'hmm, hmm, hmm' in rapid succession. That can make the interviewee feel that they're boring or that the journalist is trying to hurry you up, or bring what you are saying to a close.

Another technique is interrupting answers to questions as they are being delivered. This can be justifiable if the subject is veering off the question but people who are not used to it can react badly and become flustered. Ultimately, these techniques can affect the messages that you send out. If you react badly to this kind of stress, and remember it could take part in a live interview, it's important to know in advance. So it is important to be prepared for a variety of different styles.

Watch out for assertions

Some questions are bold and call on you to accept or deny a particular proposition. They can be particularly hard to handle in a live interview situation. For example, 'This latest management restructuring *will* mean cuts in jobs, won't it?'. Now, it may be that this is true (invariably restructurings mean someone being shown the door) but, for other reasons (lack of consultation, for example), you may not wish to confirm or deny it. It's important to know what message you will send out during the interview and to anticipate which denials you are likely to have to deal with.

That's just news sneaking up on you

Unless you take part in a live interview, very little of what you have to say will be reported. When you think that you are likely to say roughly 180 words a minute a 30-minute interview will mean you saying over 5000 words. It's rare to see features in local newspapers which are longer than 500 words. That means a lot of what you say will be ignored. It also means that some of what you say at the beginning could end up next to what you've said at the end. Journalists with good listening skills will be in a position to pick up inconsistencies in what you have said. Imagine two comments, one at the start of an interview, 'We are certain that we will start work on the town centre by the end of May', and at the end, 'We are reasonably sure that we will start work on the town centre by the end of May'. In practice it's easy to make this simple slip of the tongue but a journalist could use this difference to suggest that you are not quite as sure as you seem. As in, *'You said at the beginning of this interview that you "were certain" in your words that you will start work at the end of May. You've just finished saying that you're reasonably sure. The truth is that the scheme's in a mess and you really don't know when you'll start. That's the case, isn't it?'*

During a long interview it's easy to say the same thing in different ways. That's why it's critical that you're clear about what you are saying and about what you are not saying. And because the interviewee is not in control of the interview there's nothing to stop a journalist jumping around with their questions and throwing in odd questions when you are least expecting it.

As with every aspect of the interview preparation is essential. Make sure you know what you want to say and say it if necessary over and over again. Make sure you know what you don't want to say and never say it.

Watch out for Columbo

Finally, in this section, it's worth remembering that you are most likely to give away what you really think when your guard is down. The *Observer* last year devoted pages to the activities of public affairs' consultants based on conversations they had and overheard at cocktail parties. The *Columbo*, based on the American TV detective, is simply asking questions when they are least expected. It's interesting just how many people respond to questions asked on the way in to an interview (the headteacher is walking you to their room before the interview starts or at the end). You might probe on a school's financial state by commenting on the roughness of the décor.

Clearly, there is a lot to think about above and it may take a while before you recognize and can confidently apply your mind to dealing with journalists. I have set out below a six-point survival plan for handling media calls:

1. Find out what the story is

When a journalist calls they will be chasing a particular story. It may be something that will be going to committee. They may be looking for comment on something that the authority is doing. In order to put yourself in the best position possible you should try to find out as much information as you can. Keep a note of the issues they want answers to.

2. Find out what the deadline is

You need to know this otherwise you will not know how long you've got to prepare your answers. Journalists will tend to say that it's tight. They may do so simply because their experience is that council staff are not good at returning calls or answering questions. If you are able to establish a decent relationship with a journalist and you are reliable you will get a better grip on how long they really have.

3. Find out why you are being called

What does the journalist think you will add to the story? It could be that you are dealing with a paper that is going to committee in which case it's pretty obvious. However, it could equally be that they've looked elsewhere for the answer and drawn a blank and that's why they've come to you.

4. Find out, if you can, who else the journalist is talking to

Essentially, you want to know how they are going to approach the story, what angle they intend to take. A story about poor council tax payments could be about how difficult it is to collect this tax, or it could be about how poor the council is collecting the money. You'll get some clues by noting the specific questions that they are asking but if you know who else they're talking to (and the kinds of response they are getting) you will have a better grasp of the story.

5. Create thinking space

It can be difficult to remember that when you give a comment to the local media you could be reaching thousands of people. It's also easy to forget that passing remarks costs credibility. That's why it's important to think before you speak. Think about what you want to say to this audience at this time. You should have some key messages which inform your business and this is an opportunity to get them across. On some issues, you may convene short meetings to discuss how to handle the interview. The consequences of getting it wrong can be dire.

6. Say it and say no more

When you've decided your line say it and stick to it. It can be tempting to waffle on and share your innermost secrets with journalists but it is likely to lead to grief. So unless you want to use the story to announce your premature retirement stick to the script.

Nobody says you've got to answer the question

In this next section, we look at some of the ways in which you may choose not to answer questions and some of the techniques you can use to avoid facing the problems head on. Doubtless, in your work with committees and elsewhere, there will be times when it's simply not sensible to fully answer questions. And, of course, there will be times when things will emerge that you simply are unable to deal with. Some of the techniques I have drawn on are highlighted by Thouless and Thouless in *Straight and Crooked Thinking*. If you haven't read it, it's well worth a dip.

At the beginning of the book we looked at the concept of communication management. If we are to accept that it is important to consider managing communication in terms of the outcomes it creates then it must follow that we should look at relationships with the media in the same terms. If a journalist calls to set up an interview you should consider the interview in equally pragmatic terms.

First, you might argue that taking part in an interview is in itself a good thing. After all, staff in a public body ought to be able to demonstrate public accountability by being open to public scrutiny. A live radio interview, for example, can show local people, who are interested in hearing your arguments tested, that you are open to challenge. Of course, this is underpinned by an optimistic set of assumptions, that is to say, that you will be given the opportunity to lay out your arguments and to explain your side of the story in an objective way. In the main, if local government officers were given such opportunities, it's likely that it would bore the audience half to death. Journalists will, therefore, seek to put your comments into a story context. They will give meaning to what you say by making it part of something else which you will have no control over at all.

Second, you could argue that taking part in the interview will help you achieve strategic outcomes which you would otherwise have to pursue by other means. For example, you could be asked to respond to complaints on the price of leisure in your area and use the interview to stress the range of leisure activities on offer. In this case there's as much in it for you as there is for the journalist.

Finally, you could consider that taking part in the interview would not help you. Indeed, it could be that the matters under discussion are at such a delicate stage that any interview would simply damage the possibility of action behind the scenes. You will find that participants in pay discussions will often shy away from public comment as interviews may give away (to the opposition) hints about their thinking.

At the same time, the no comment can be counter-productive. It can be easily interpreted as evasiveness, or that the authority has something to hide. For that reason, it is sometimes necessary to take part in an interview while remaining committed to giving nothing away. This section looks at some of the techniques which can be employed to avoid dealing with this question. Clearly, when they are used they can cause listeners (and readers) to judge that you are avoiding the question. However, it is possible, even on live radio and television, to give the impression of openness while simultaneously remaining closed.

Open to question

Questions are very powerful things. They focus attention on certain aspects of knowledge (the bits that appear in the question itself) and necessarily limit the meaning of the response. Like clever barristers, journalists can steer interviewees through a mass of knowledge without ever touching the parts that you may want to deal with. This section is about some of the techniques which can be used to reset the context, create opportunities to speak outside the question and increase the chances of getting what you want covered in the media.

Making a statement irrespective of the question

This is where you are absolutely clear about what you want to say. It might be used when you feel you need to appear to be available to talk to the media but you want to say no more than absolutely necessary.

For example:

'Do you think you have enough money to properly finance your school?'

'We believe that this school has gone from strength to strength in the last five years and we are confident that both the school and our pupils will continue to thrive.'

Questioning the assumptions in the question

Every question is rooted in assumptions. If you are to question the assumptions you need to quickly identify what those assumptions are.

Key point

Clearly, you can be bold and simply say, 'I don't want to answer that question; I want to answer this question' but that approach is likely to cause the journalist to simply pull you back to the question. However, it is possible to focus attention on one particular aspect of the subject under discussion as a way of leading the interview into new territory.

For example:

'Do you think that you have enough money to properly finance your school?'

'The key point here is are we happy with the quality of education in our school and I think the answer has to be "yes"'.

Take the question:

'Would you not accept that too much public money is being wasted on sustaining the privileges of those in high office?'

The answer could focus on 'too much', what is meant by 'public money', 'waste', or 'privileges'.

One response might be:

'It is easy to focus on the amount of public money spent. Surely it is vital that we look at what results we get by spending that money and if you look closely at our track record in achievement you will find ...'

Questioning the credibility of the interviewer

This depends on knowing your subject well. Journalists, unless they are specialists, tend to have a skating understanding of the issues they are writing about. They will rely on executive summaries and cursory research rather than detailed investigation. That can easily be turned to your advantage. This technique can be irritating to the interviewer as it undermines them but it can be useful for one-off escapes.

For example:

> 'In a recent government report on the use of public money it was accepted that 25 per cent of all committee spending plans needed closer scrutiny by outside parties, would you not accept that this area needs to be looked at more closely in your authority?'

> 'I think that's an interesting question but if you look closely at the report you'll find that's not the main point the authors were trying to make and that was this: ...'

Questioning the evidence

The same technique can be applied to the citing of any evidence. Evidence-gathering often depends upon taking assertions, testing them in a sample, ensuring a degree of reliability and generalizing on that basis. All conclusions are cautious and couched in caveats and that creates room for manoeuvre. Everything can be questioned.

For example:

> 'New research shows that working people are under more stress than ever before and that this is leading a to a new class of white-collar industrial accidents, isn't it time something was done about this?'

> 'I have seen the research and found it interesting but we should be careful not to make too much of research which was carried out in another country and in only two professions. However, there are some key points we should be looking at and they are ...'

Recontextualizing the question

This is a selling routine. Basically, you use your answer to a question to try to show the journalist that the question you think they ought to ask is better than the one that they have asked. Success depends upon two things: how well you sell your alternative; and whether they're determined (having heard your response) to ask you the original question anyway.

For example:

> 'Do you think that stress is causing some of the country's best executives to retire early?'

'That's an interesting point but I think we should really be looking at why we're spending as much time talking about stress at the moment. I think there's an obsession with finding scapegoats. The fact is that if you look at the investment track record in British industry, or if you consider the power of imports, or whatever, they all give you a different understanding of the apparent malaise in industry. We would do better to look at the big picture.'

Moving the interview into emotional territory

It is possible to redefine the problem outlined in a question in a different emotional state. If you consider how those listening to what you have to say will be feeling and how you might want them to feel, you can use different words to signal a change of mood.

For example:

'Would you not agree that your council's policy of closing swimming pools at weekends is going to result in a poorer service?'

'I think we shouldn't forget how swimmers feel here. We have spoken to those people who use our pool and they believe that it is better to open the pool for fewer hours and to use the money saved to provide a better service. I think we should listen to them. After all, if we let down those people who currently support our service what hope have we in winning the confidence of those who don't?'.

Employing common sense to win an argument

It is likely, unless the journalist has carried out a substantial amount of research, that some of their questions will be rooted in common sense. They may say, for example, that the fact that you intend to increase the council tax will be rejected by the whole community. Of course, they will not have carried out the research, but will rely instead on common sense to substantiate their question. The same technique can be applied in reverse.

For example:

'Surely you can't be deaf to the fact that the prospect of putting up your council tax yet again has the whole community shouting "no"?'

'I don't hear those words. What I hear is people who say "We want better services" and we're listening to that. I hear people say, "We want value for money" and we're listening to that. And, most of all, I hear people say, "You don't get a decent service unless you spend a decent amount of money". And we've heard that loud and clear.'

Suggesting that the journalist has an agenda

This is a risky strategy. Basically, it involves appealing to the audience to recognize that you, as the interviewee, are not being given a fair trial. You can overtly, or covertly, suggest that the journalist has some kind of motive in taking a particular line of questioning.

For example:

'Surely you can't be deaf to the fact that the prospect of putting up your council tax yet again has the whole community shouting "no"?'

'I wonder why you say this. There can be no question that it's in the interests of a commercial station to prey on potential conflict between the council and our community. Clearly, it's good for your station and in quiet news times it might just keep people listening but I think it would be better if we all moved beyond this and looked at ways in which we can work together for the good of our community. That is why I think we should be trying to find ways of better explaining how we spend the money entrusted to us by local people. That is where we should be focused, not on contrived and artificial conflict.'

Using rhetorical devices to win audience attention

If we make what we are saying interesting enough we will attract attention to our message. Of course, during national television interviews, this is more difficult as journalists and audiences are more familiar with this technique but it can, nonetheless, be a powerful way of delivering your message. In the section on sound-bites we have outlined some of the ways in which you can package your message. The same techniques, of repetition, three-part lists and so on, can be applied in response to a question.

For example:

'Would you not agree that your authority already spends too much money on salaries and, therefore, should be thinking about cutting pay not increasing it?'

'It's important to put this in context. Our proposals are about value. We value our staff. We value the work they do and local people value them, too. Our latest research shows that year on year our communities think we do a better and better job. We all know that in the end the price of something depends upon the value that you place on it and that is why we will be saying to our staff that we, and the community, value them very much indeed.'

However, it is always important to weigh up the costs and benefits of avoiding questions. It is always possible to avoid answering questions but that has to be done knowing the consequences of doing so. Remember that every action could have an impact on your most valuable asset, your reputation. That might mean your personal reputation or it might be that of your authority. But it is critical that if you are to protect this asset you need to bear in mind the possible negative impacts of taking evasive action. All of our actions in public bodies are ultimately shaped by what the public requires of us. The public alone will judge our worth.

Look ahead. There can be little doubt that public bodies will be required to be freer with information, to be more open and accountable about their actions. Local authorities will be required to consult and involve citizens in their activities. Truth is a vital commodity in those dealings and if an authority is to successfully manage partnerships then it will need to think about how it is perceived in the various marketplaces in which it will operate. That, too, will depend on honesty with yourself.

At the same time, it is important to recognize that we do not live in an ideal world and that the management of information is a tool which will help bring about desired outcomes. That means learning how the thing works and using it to the advantage of your authority.

There are, of course, times when there is an excessive amount of media attention focused on an organization. In such circumstances those who are involved have to weather a storm which may last for many months. Mike McCabe who was communications officer with Gloucester City Council during the Fred West period experienced the full force of a media onslaught and in this final section he tells us about it by focusing on one day.

Of course, few middle managers will ever be faced with this process as a part of their normal work, but there are principles from this day's work that can be applied to the everyday business of message management.

Case study: 'Alarm calls', by Mike McCabe, Head of Communications, Chester City Council, previously Communications Officer, Gloucester City Council

6.00 am on a Friday morning. It's dark, it's pouring with rain and I am struggling to get dressed following a phone call telling me that a leak to the *Daily Express* has blown our story, due to be announced on Monday, that the city council is to buy, demolish and 'turn to dust' the house at 25 Cromwell Street. A well-planned operation to pre-brief the local media, members and others, has itself been turned to dust by the leak. I have no interest in who leaked it, I must focus on the national media pack who will, even now, be on the road to Gloucester baying for stories and waking everyone up to get them.

6.30 am in the office. My name is mud with all of the local media who are very unhappy that the exclusive they thought they would have on Monday is no more. They are all blaming each other for the leak. I do several interviews on the hoof to mollify them. Phone calls are coming in thick and fast from the UK and European media. We will never satisfy all the requests for interviews, pictures and information and must get control quickly. A hurriedly drafted press release gives the bare bones of the story and announces a 10 am press conference. It goes out to anyone and everyone and gives us the breathing space to do the essentials – think, plan and act.

My colleagues in the police press office are being besieged with calls but our pre-planning is paying off. Our agreed line of, it's a city council operation, is used to good effect. At the same time the planned 24 hours of police guard on the house is brought in three days early – never underestimate what the media will do for a story – we must ensure that no souvenirs can be taken and the police guard will do that.

My mind goes back to the organized chaos of the massive press conference held at the end of the trial of Rose West in Winchester. Today will not be on the same scale but we still need to provide facilities for TV, radio, the press and photographers – both at the conference and in Cromwell Street. We have two hours in which to do so and to prepare ourselves for the press conference.

We set up a media log, we close off the council car park and an all day conference in the civic suite is hurriedly moved. Decisions are taken at the speed of light. What the media reports tonight and tomorrow is crucial to the success of our operation, hence the needs of the media must take absolute priority.

Previous guidance for officers and members to always refer Cromwell Street enquiries to myself pays off in that they decline to speak to the many journalists ringing them. But this causes me a headache because they keep ringing me to say they've been contacted! One person is asked to ring round everybody to tell them what is going on and what to do. We must eliminate the chance of a journalist getting an off the cuff comment which gives them a great story but damages our communications objectives. Some people are simply told not to answer their phones!

8.30 am I will be part of the press conference – but not in the jeans and jumper I am wearing and breakfast would be nice – no food means no straight thinking and lots of mistakes. The five minute journey to home takes 20 minutes as I stop to take several calls on the mobile and give advice and direction to the support team – earlier we had arranged support to take my calls, make notes and deal with practical preparations which is essential.

Once home I rush breakfast and then enjoy a new experience of taking a bath while I continue to take phone calls on the mobile – don't drop it!

The adrenaline needed for success is really pumping as I return to the office, but I must remember to slow down and think. Many journalists ring to say that they can't make the press conference. They are demanding immediate interviews on the phone or down the line. If we say yes then the press conference will become a non-event and those attending will rightly feel cheated. We say no, not till later and I get called some very uncomplimentary things.

9.45 am. Calm before the storm. Taking just five minutes off to think and plan is essential because the journalists waiting for us will be prepared and, if we are unprepared, things could go pear-shaped.

A closed room with the chief executive, leader and myself. What are our objectives? What are we going to say? Who will deal with what? I remind them of the basics: don't respond to questions thrown as we walk in. Let me do the introductions and set the ground rules. Don't take papers in because you will just fiddle with them and look nervous. Look straight out at your audience or, if you aren't speaking, look at your colleague who is and nod in support of the points he is making. Ignore any distractions, cameras will move, microphones will appear and disappear and the journalists will talk to each other loudly. Finally, when it is over, don't hang around for a chat!

10.00 am. The press conference. Remember the rules. Get them sat down, walk in together, keep control, say what you want to, answer the questions, keep an eye out for traps and deflect them. We know we are doing the right thing, but we still have to watch out for 'waste of taxpayers' money', 'why not a museum?', 'is Gloucester a sick city', etc.

The conference ends and everyone wants one-to-one interviews. I carefully note the questions because if there are any nasty surprises they are likely to come here – no journalist will want to share their line with others.

10.45 am. It's over. Now an endless round of interviews over the phone to national radio and press before we must refocus on the local media and their lunchtime needs.

11.00 am. The day has hardly started. The next seven hours will be filled with more of the same, thinking, planning, analysing, acting and reacting. Only then can we start to plan for Monday when the demolition will begin.

6 am Saturday morning. No alarm calls. The coverage achieved is worth our efforts. We were caught out but moved quickly to catch up. That is the key to success.

Few people reading this book will be the eye of an international media storm but the lessons are the same for small as well as big stories. Think carefully through the situation and be prepared for the full range of activities that will arise.

The fact is that local government is a public service and will, therefore, increasingly take place under the public gaze. The public expects the media to tell them what is going on and any local authority that tries to defend against that will not achieve that isolation. New local government will be more and more open and, therefore, successful managers will recognize and welcome that openness.

6 Getting your message covered

I will begin this chapter by looking briefly at the factors which affect local news coverage followed by an exercise that concerns the selection of news for a local paper. I will then go on to examine ways of engaging journalists in news from your council and in finding ways of thinking like a journalist. I will look first at calling journalists, then at press releases. Finally, I will consider media briefings and press conferences.

News is a product. While it may reach consumers neatly packaged, nicely laid out and well-written it has already been processed, for the most part, by the time it reaches the journalist who writes it. As a product news is rarely the reproduction of events as they happen. Just as the vegetables we buy in the supermarket look as if they have arrived naturally straight from the field but are, in fact, the result of a complex process of production, so it is for news. News is a product of a series of information-gathering and processing systems.

If a journalist had to go out and actually observe everything that was reported it would take a whole day's work for a handful of journalists to give you just one story and since all news media give you a variety of stories on a day-to-day basis, we know that this is not the case. News producers rely on getting their material from reliable, credible sources.

LOCAL NEWS COVERAGE

The sources for most of the local news we consume are as follows:

The police

Crime is a staple in the news diet and the police will ensure that local news media are well-fed on crime events and how they are being handled.

The courts

This is the other end of the judicial system. Most local papers will regularly send journalists to the local court.

Local councils

The council is an important source of news which affects local people. Journalists will be dispatched to cover committee and council meetings. They will have access to regular agenda papers and will have a network of sources within the council to help them understand any unclear agenda items. Also, councils will regularly send out press releases to the local media.

Local hospitals

They will pass on information about health disasters, illnesses, etc.

Press Association, Reuters

Sources of news which are happening nationally.

Other news media

Journalists will scan other news media for possible stories. An item, which begins on national radio, will have a local angle somewhere.

Reliable sources

Reporters with particular patches to cover (such as crime, politics, business or local government) will know about stories which are coming up, about future trends, issues and the like.

Government sources

The government is a major source of news. Journalists can scan the Internet for sources of news from the Central Office of Information.

Phone calls to the media

For local government (and other parts of the public sector) this is an important area of business. Aggrieved council taxpayers will often take their grievances straight to the media. Often armed with limited and (misunderstood) scant facts the media will pursue officers for 'the truth'. All too often it's a more complex picture than that painted by the complainant.

Events

And then there are events – things which happen locally and elsewhere.

If you think what these different sources produce in your locality, inevitably there will be more news than there is space to report it. One of the first jobs the editorial team of a news product will have to do will be to select what gets in and what's left out. In making this decision journalists will be affected by a number of criteria. The following exercise examines some of those criteria by imagining for a moment that you are looking at the prospects at a morning editorial meeting.

 Exercise – prospects

You are on the editorial team of a local daily newspaper. Imagine that the paper is based in Weston-super-Mare. Some of the stories are concerned with Weston and say so. Others are based nearby in Bristol. If you are not sure where either of those places are have a look at a map and use that to judge whether you think your readers will be interested in some of the stories under consideration.

Your paper, the *Daily Trumpet*, is targeting local people who are married with responsibilities. Your task is to select the top five stories for the paper. Those are stories which you think will be most interesting to your readers.

It is mid-June. The World Cup is in its second week. This is a mid-week paper.

1. Government to introduce new legislation on soccer violence
2. Weston: man wins tickets to World Cup Final
3. Bristol: car crash driver was 12 years old
4. North Somerset: council to introduce by-law to curb drinking in street
5. Weston: youth crime goes up by 12 per cent says police report
6. South East: tourism set to fall by 10 per cent says local survey
7. London: Earl Spencer in new row over Diana memorial
8. Children: television is new child minder says Bristol University survey
9. Louise Woodward: new survey says she should still be in US prison

10. Weston: local businesses to hold conference on supporting summer visitors
11. Football: Shearer says, 'We can go all the way'
12. Weston: former Mayor questioned by police on expense claims
13. Bristol: ten couples to celebrate Golden Weddings
14. Bristol: three boats collide in Channel
15. SouthWest: M5 busiest motorway in Europe – new figures
16. London: Blair EU Presidency gets high ratings in a Euro survey
17. Bristol: third night of violence on housing estate – five injuries
18. Electronic business to grow by 25 per cent in next six months – CBI survey
19. Survey: North East children do worse than comparable South East in school
20. Swindon: two youths arrested following World Cup ticket scam
21. Oxford: Birmingham nine-year-old gets MA
22. Weston: we've no faith in council to bring in tourists say local hoteliers
23. Bristol judge says we need to get tough on fraud in the public sector
24. Weston: council leader says, 'We'll crack down on work-shy staff'
25. London: coolest capital in Europe says Weather Centre
26. Weston: local college set to open European studies course
27. Weston: two primary schools to close
28. Weston: parents plan to march on council following planned school closures
29. Los Angeles: sextuplets born to teenagers
30. Bristol: 10-year-old drowns in Channel
31. Glasgow: 'friendliest city in Europe' says international survey
32. Orkney: locals fear undeclared oil spills
33. London: pound value set to fall by 8 per cent by 2010
34. Bristol: fire chief says hoax calls have fallen following local campaign
35. Weston: new councillor says overwork is making life fall apart
36. Reuters: suspected war crimes in former Yugoslavia
37. New book claims Brown wants to be Prime Minister
38. Weston: fire in supermarket was arson says senior police source
39. Birmingham: six councillors banned from public office following fraud scandal
40. Weston: town centre car crash – no injuries

What got in?

The prospects exercise is often used in training events and, in the main, the following factors tend to determine the best news.

Is it local?

If it's done in Weston then Weston gets in, Bristol next and the rest of the country comes a poor third.

Does it affect our readers?

The school closure stories tend to get selected because readers will have children at school and will tend to be worried about these things.

How many readers does it affect?

There will be stories which affect readers but only affect a few. The Herald of Free Enterprise disaster received a lot of attention not only because it was a disaster in which many British people died but also because many people *could* have been on that (or another) ship. France is a popular holiday destination. Similarly, in local government there will be some policies which will affect many people.

How big an event is it?

If it involves the loss of life it tends to get selected even if it is not local. Death comes first, then serious injuries and then the rest.

Does it involve a high-status person?

Participants, when probed, said they would select the Bristol housing estate story if it involved someone famous, like a visiting pop star or someone royal.

Is it bad news?

By and large, bad news tends to get selected over good news. The worse the news the better. Another way of looking at this is whether it breaks with the norm.

Is it an anniversary?

The media will focus on stories or anniversaries.

Is it quirky or a human interest story?

Good news will tend to get selected if it has a nice human side to it. This, combined with something unusual, will get selected. So while some participants will select the World Cup story (even though it involved only two people) they wouldn't select lottery win stories (which aren't featured) because it happens too frequently these days.

However, if your council is to be a good source of news it is important that you understand the kinds of story which will interest the media. The above exercise should help readers understand something of selecting news items but given the number of potential stories which emerge from a council, officers and members should think about how to manage information to the council's advantage.

Councils are open to public scrutiny. This means that from the minute news becomes public it should be open to others' interpretation. If news management is to be maximized to the council's advantage then you must first be aware of the ways in which people think and, more importantly, the ways in which the media think.

MANAGING INFORMATION TO YOUR ADVANTAGE

Committees, where decisions are officially made, are by and large open. A journalist will know any week what decisions are likely to be taken simply by looking at the public committee papers or agendas. And where middle managers do not appreciate this fact before the papers go out they can often find themselves dealing reactively with something which could easily have been planned for in advance.

As the agenda for meetings is being put together officers will often sit down with the chair of the particular committee or subcommittee and plan the agenda. They will know what decisions have to be made. They will be aware of the various conversations the chair may have to engage in in advance of the committee in order to win support for the particular proposal. In the same way as a chair may have to sell their ideas to their colleagues and build support and, therefore, manage information, so they can use the same thinking in relation to the press.

PLANNING THE AGENDA WITH AN EYE TO THE MESSAGE IN THE MEDIA

Nearly everybody who writes committee papers has a simple agenda of getting their recommendations agreed so that they can carry on with their work. Consequently, very few of them have an eye to what the media might make of the papers they have written and how they might impact upon a journalist in search of a story. If you are responsible for either compiling a single paper or, moreover, a whole agenda, then it is essential to 'read' the papers and the agenda with a media eye. It is simply not possible to expect the full-time communications manager in the local authority to carry out this role. It must become a normal task of the middle manager. It's important to think of the items on a committee paper both in terms of what you would want to achieve through the media as well as what will interest them. You might apply a number of simple tests to each item.

How will what we are proposing affect people?

The local media are interested in what happens to groups of local people. Think back to the section on news values. If you are going to do something which will make a big difference to local people then that will increase its interest value. For example, you may be proposing to invest thousands of pounds in after-school care which will mean that hundreds of children will now get access to a life-improvement opportunity.

It might be that what you propose will represent a significant change in policy or direction. Again, for example, you might have previously rejected the banning of beef from school menus but you are now proposing to introduce a blanket ban. That will affect a significant number of people and, therefore, will be of interest.

Is it business as usual or new business?

The media will tend to focus on events that have happened or are about to happen. Does that apply to what you are proposing to do?

Does it involve an area of controversy?

If what you are proposing is likely to ruffle any senior management or political feathers then it will probably interest the media, too. It may affect local businesses or local partners. All the obvious areas will attract controversy. Are you about to do something where you could be accused of wasting money? Are you going to upset any important local people or special interest groups? Are you going to make a foray into the private lives of others and confirm the 'nanny state' idea of taking children away from their natural parents and so on?

How does it sit with existing stereotypes?

Remember that you will not be seen in a positive light by the media. Local government is often seen negatively. Think of the dominant stories which are logged in public consciousness. They're about the slowness of bureaucracy, loony left councils taking decisions that fly in the face of local common sense; more recently fraud and corruption. Journalists will, therefore, be attracted to stories which reinforce those stereotypes.

I came across an instance of a local authority that decided to ban a council tenant from using his Christmas tree lights because they offended a neighbour. In some ways the decision was entirely reasonable. The person concerned had covered virtually every square inch of his house with lights. It was like the Blackpool illuminations and it kept his neighbours awake, but the minute the council reached its decision they were dealing with calls from the *Daily Star*. And it made the front page the next day.

Is there a running story?

Often the media will be interested in what you are doing, even if it appears insignificant, because it is part of a running story. Decisions around the activities of travellers, for example, will usually attract attention. Local authority decisions around travellers are always fraught with problems mainly because there's no easy answer. When travellers arrive there's usually nowhere for them to go. So they will settle where they're not wanted (as the media will describe it).

From then on it's like a long run at the West End. Enter party one: local residents, 'We don't want them here'. Party two: the council, 'We want to do all we can'. Party three: others on the council who think the council is being too soft. Party four: the media speaking up for local people, and so on.

It's an excellent story for the media because as the plot unfolds there are many twists and turns. The council may take action against the travellers so the media can turn up at court. There will be the eviction – a photo opportunity in itself. There is the crime element – there are always accusations about an increase in the crime rate – and this may have nothing to do with the travellers. There will be the clear-up after the travellers have left. Then there will be the financial burden – the council meets the bill. The travellers may simply move along the road and the whole process starts again.

Think what this story is like to a journalist. Once it starts they know they have a story for many weeks and all they have to do is get the different players in the story to say their lines in the correct sequence. The journalist relays the lines to other members of the cast and away goes the story again. Hundreds of words, week after week.

Does it involve important players?

It's easy to deal with the activities of councils if you are able to reduce it to the activities of personalities. Take the case of Coventry City Council where the council proposed to move the Museum of British Road Transport as part of a rethink of the city centre. Although there appeared to be unanimous support for the proposal from the leading group, one councillor stood out against it. His proposal was that the Museum should stay where it was. He so effectively mustered his arguments that he won the support of the local media. The story then changed from being about moving a museum to being a battle of bureaucracy against common sense. In the end, common sense won, by a mile and the Museum stayed where it was.

Thereafter, that particular councillor attracted media attention (in fact he had done so before the Museum battle). If you have councillors or officers who are in the public eye you will need take that into account at the pre-agenda stage.

Does it fly in the face of common sense?

I have considered elsewhere the importance of common sense as a means of understanding the complexities of everyday life. Councils will act often in the face of common sense. There was a recent story where a council banned an Al Jolsen impersonator from 'blacking-up' for his show. In the event, he came on stage, was booed by theatre-goers, who were looking forward to seeing a blacked-up Al Jolsen impersonator and he was forced to put his make-up on. What started as a discussion between the director of leisure and his colleagues ended up on national radio. It was difficult for the council to appear anything other than silly.

It's not that their actions weren't in some way correct. They were after all trying to be sensitive to the needs of those who might have been offended by a white man pretending to be a black man. The problem was what they did about it. Had they considered the outcome – the council looking politically correct, out of touch and part of the 'nanny state' – they might have considered an alternative course of action. Middle managers need to be aware that the common reaction of most local authorities to a lot of people's activities is to try and stop them from doing them. By the end of this century this instinct to regulate activity is out of tune with a lot of people's common sense and banning people from wearing make-up appears weird.

Have you looked at what you are doing through other people's eyes?

What journalists do, and do well, is to look at stories through other people's eyes. A local newspaper, which is trying to reach *married people with responsibilities*, will consider events from their point of view. Local government has a harder job to do. There are many different constituencies of interest. It's easy to please one group while grossly offending another and that makes it a challenge. However, it is important to try to think about how what you will do might be represented.

Crucially, poor or critical coverage might not just produce a headache to the council. It might actually cause it to take a different course of action than the one it had planned but put to one side. Whatever journalists dig up for themselves or you inadvertently or proactively tell them, there will still be a rich seam of news for them to mine.

UNDERSTANDING HOW TO GET COVERAGE —
INTERNALIZING NEWS VALUES

The more you understand the ways that journalists think the better chance you have of getting your news covered on your terms. When you can second-guess not only what story they will find attractive, but also how they are likely to approach it (in terms of who they will speak to, what kinds of questions they will ask and so on) you will be better prepared. That means that when they come to talk to you about something you're involved in you'll have a better idea about how to approach the issue. The next section focuses on understanding how journalists think and how middle managers can use that knowledge to get their stories in the media.

SELLING YOUR STORIES TO THE MEDIA

It can be a lot easier to talk to journalists about something which might interest them than simply sending a press release. It will give you an instant reaction although, if a journalist is interested in what you are saying, they may ask for further information and at that point you would send a press release. However, there is a fear of journalists, which runs through every level of local government.

It's probably based on watching too much *Newsnight* and looking at the way that Jeremy Paxman savages his interviewees night after night. If the local authority manager is going to talk to a number of journalists a lot then it is vital that the manager gets to know the individuals involved. It is not recommended that the manager must become friends with them, but it is a very good idea to remove the fantasy from your mind about journalists. For this reason alone it is vital for the manager to create a relationship.

There are some points you should remember before you pick up the phone:

Understand their problems

Local government senior managers are not the only ones with problems. You may be faced with strenuous demands from your employer and people down the corridor who want your job. So are journalists.

There is an ambitious stream running through all local media. Just about everyone who is part of a national media began in either a local paper or a local radio station. It's where they learn their trade and, more importantly, it's where they earn their stripes. Ambitious journalists need to mark themselves out from the herd. That means being first with the news, being prolific or finding out what's really happening on their patch.

You, of course, can help them. Providing that you know that the hand which feeds them will get bitten from time to time, you can develop a relationship with them, which will be mutually beneficial.

However, not everyone is ambitious and the cost-cutting, getting more for less, which pervades local government, is alive and well in the local media. When the axe is poised to fall (and that might be a permanent state), journalists need to be able to show that they've delivered. Stories, stories, stories. The media do not want to publish or broadcast when they've filled a programme or a paper. There will be a news programme in local radio on the hour, every hour and there may be several issues of your local paper every day. They need to be filled. The pressure to keep on producing stories is always there.

Turn problems into opportunities

Everyone's problem is someone else's opportunity. A journalist with a hole to fill is an opportunity for your story. So it's important to remember that there may be space for your message simply because it's all they've got. There will be times when the media will simply print your press release wholesale. Again, as often as not, this will reflect the pressure they are under to fill the page. Of course, they won't just print any old thing. The fact that you got covered will have something to do with the fact that councils are credible organizations and, hopefully, your release was reasonably well written.

Sell for a reason

Getting media coverage in itself is not particularly difficult. If you simply want to get your name in the papers, then have a rake around in those cupboards which you keep all of your skeletons in. Yes, you would get column inches but you would not necessarily gain as an organization (unless it was part of a planned clean-up operation).

So it's crucial that it's part of a communication strategy. It should, in some way, incrementally take you towards your agreed objectives. Communication is a management tool – no matter what you are doing. When you are taking recommendations to a particular committee, the way that may be reported could affect the decision taken by members. You need to know about those implications in advance.

Help the media

Recognizing the importance of other people's agendas is critical to success in any enterprise. So if you have a local radio station, which is trying to reach young people, why not ensure that they get your 'Youth Strategy' press release first or, better, talk to them about ways in which they might be able to work with you to engage local young people. That way they get closer to their audience and you appear more interesting by virtue of an association with a 'happening' station.

Get the timing right

Good timing is crucial in any walk of life but in industries where business is fundamentally time-driven, getting it wrong will put you back many steps. Every media outlet is run to deadlines. Unless a local paper preplanned when stories would need to be finished, laid out and printed you'd never see the paper in the shops. So it's vital that you know when the deadlines are and to remember never to phone a journalist around deadline time unless they've asked you to, or unless something catastrophic has happened in your office in the last five minutes.

It may seem a small thing but if you are phoning a journalist at their most stressful time, you'll be signalling not only a lack of understanding of the way they operate, but also a disregard for *their* priorities.

Eat, drink, sleep (the media)

Media coverage is about getting your specific messages to specific audiences for a particular purpose. That approach will mean getting to know which media reach which audience. Before you even think of calling a journalist from a particular media outlet you should know their product. Doing so will give you invaluable market information – how they approach stories, who they target, their approach, the issues they lead on, key writers and so on.

The better you know the media you are dealing with the easier it is to deal with them. One of the obvious and better ways of achieving this is by being aware of what media you like to look at, read or listen to. What attracts you to a story and why?

How did they use your ideas?

If you've sold your idea to a particular journalist it's worth looking at how it has been used. Say you've given them a story on how your council intends to save money through staff ideas, find out who they've spoken to. How did they follow it up? How long did it take them? Were they thorough?

All of this information will give you feedback, which you can use the next time you pick up the phone to talk to them, and it will give you food for thought on other areas they may be interested in.

Face to face

Getting face to face with journalists is important. Getting to know them, understanding what drives them as people and knowing their approach will all help you. Yes, you'll need to be careful about what you say. A successful working rule is never to say anything which you would mind seeing in print. If you want to confess your sins don't do so over a pint with the local political editor, see a priest.

However, it's worth remembering, and if necessary checking, the conventions about being 'on the record'. When you're on the record anything you say may be quoted and attributed to you. When you're off the record anything you say may be quoted but not attributed. You will come across 'sources close to ...' and the like when the source is off the record. If you don't want to appear anywhere near the story but you want to get coverage, then send documents from wayward post-boxes or make sure you spread your message through the gossip network. This process has usually been connected with leaking documents from an organization in such a way as to cause it embarrassment. In fact, organizations can choose to release information this way because it adds extra spice to the news if it comes via a brown envelope rather than in public. So as part of a strategy, organizations can selectively leak very usefully.

Tomorrow's news

Think ahead. There will be papers to fill tomorrow and programmes will be broadcast. Where is your organization going? What kind of media coverage would benefit you? What of the journalists you are dealing with? What do they want? How can you help them, by developing ideas, giving them access to thinking or sharing information, achieve what they want?

Negotiate and get favours in the bank

At its root the relationship between source and journalist is symbiotic. You each need each other. The council is an important source of local news and the local news media are the key to effective mass communication. Any symbiotic relationship is a trading arrangement. As long as you remain useful to each other then you'll continue to trade but the price of trade should not mean the loss of stock elsewhere.

For example, you might have a good working relationship with the local business correspondent. You might give her a regular source of good stories. Her editor will be happy as she will be. You might be negotiating a difficult deal with a local partnership when it goes wrong and it reaches the ears of your journalist contact. You could be tempted to say to the journalist that it would be better if she didn't publish the story.

However, she will need to make a judgement – do the benefits of holding back on the story outweigh the disbenefits of her editor thinking that she should go with it anyway. This is worsened in a competitive media situation. If there are several media outlets who hear this story she may be forced to go with it anyway, otherwise her paper's credibility will be compromised by your arrangement.

Critically, then, it's a negotiated relationship. It's also about realising that a bad press doesn't mean you can't still be friends with the local media. Yet, there are many stories of councils 'taking their ball away' when they get a succession of bad stories. It's better to be talking and negotiating than to shut the door and get hammered by bad coverage.

Of course, you may not wish to talk to the media directly. There are a number of well-established techniques, which will make it easier to get the kind of coverage you want, and they are as follows:

- press releases;
- media briefings;
- news conferences;
- photo opportunities.

Press releases

A press release is a news story written from your point of view. It involves setting out the facts, and saying why they matter, in a way which makes it as easy as possible to interest the journalist in what you are saying. Paradoxically, although it is the established way of selling your story and the form journalists are most likely to respond to, it is also for that reason, in practical terms, most fraught with difficulties. Whereas a telephone call will allow you to establish a relationship and let you know by virtue of the reaction you are getting whether your story is interesting to a journalist, the press release simply goes into the newsroom and you wait.

Newsrooms get thousands of press releases every week and what that means is that each will get a very small amount of attention. One particular news editor I know says that she would give each less than five seconds. What's more he said that if he recognizes the typeface or the layout of the envelope (and knows that it comes from a particular council) she doesn't even bother to open the envelope. It goes straight in the bin. And when a journalist says that he will only give a release five seconds attention that does not mean that he will put it to one side and consider it later. Journalists do not usually add press releases to their reading pile. A press release is a once-only opportunity. If you don't get attention the first time, then you will have to find another means of selling your story and that's why your release has to combine an understanding of news values, which were covered earlier in the chapter, with the use of a very specific form.

A press release should look like a press release. The conventions are very straightforward, established and easy to use and yet it is surprising how few people actually use them. For some reason, it seems strange that many people, trying to sell their story to the media, seem to want to force journalists to take news on their terms, rather than making it as easy as possible to interest them.

So here are the conventions of a press release:

- it should say 'news release' or 'news from' at the top;
- it should say what your organization is;
- it should look as though your release paper is established – hand-written notes simply convince journalists that you don't know what you're doing;
- it should be dated – with today's date;
- it should have a clear headline which encapsulates the story;
- the first paragraph should tell the story and answer five key questions (who?, what?, where?, when? and why?);
- subsequent paragraphs should add facts and opinions to the story;
- it should quote key players – people who have a legitimate contribution to make;
- quotes should be written as though they have been spoken;
- it should be typed, double-spaced or a space-and-a-half;
- it should be on one or two sides of A4 paper;
- technical detail or explanatory remarks should be saved for the 'notes to editors' which are after the main release;
- when it is ended it should say 'ends';
- it should give a phone number of where you can be reached and if you may be reached out of hours, where you can be contacted.

I have set out on page 114 an example of what your release should look like.

So why the conventions? We now look at them in a bit more depth.

The importance of the overall form

If you are to be taken seriously from the outset, you need to be able to convince the person at the other end of the fax that you know the business. They don't know you from Adam and what's more, they don't necessarily believe that just because you work for a local authority you know what you're doing. That surprises many people. Using the conventions shows them that you, at least, understand something. As you will see from the news editor's perspective (in Chapter 8) some journalists don't hold local government in high regard.

EXAMPLE – PRESS RELEASE

PUT THE DATE IN
29 June 2000

HEADLINE – GET THEIR ATTENTION

COUNCIL LEADER SAYS STAFF MUST PROVE PRODUCTIVITY

PARA 1: TELL THE STORY
A council leader today said that local authority staff would have to prove their productivity if they expected job security.

PARA 2: PUT IT IN CONTEXT
Copeland Council Leader, Jack Smith, speaking at a Business Link conference, said: 'Local government spends £75 billion nationally. We spend £75 million in this area. Local people have the right to know that they are getting a decent return on that money.'

PARA 3: TELL THEM WHAT YOU THINK
Councillor Smith added: 'We expect Marks & Spencer to give us value for money. It's time that local government asked itself to pass the same tests that we all use as consumers. I believe that staff will get more job satisfaction if they know that they've given their pound of flesh'.

PARA 4: MORE FACTS, MORE VIEWS
'The public sector is the biggest employer, the largest service provider and under continuous public scrutiny and yet we fail in most people's minds most of the time. If we are able to say "value for money" and mean it then we'll all go up in people's estimation and that can only be a good thing.'

TELL THEM IT'S FINISHED
Ends

TELL THEM HOW TO GET MORE INFORMATION
For further information please call Sam Bucket on 01 946 392392

There is a lot of pressure, particularly on junior officers, not to use the conventions. Senior managers, who at times believe that dealing with the media is somehow dirty, will signal this by sending out news releases on their own terms and, as we all know, if you look as though you are not compromising, that is how it is read. If you don't want coverage don't send out press releases. If you do, play the game. Tell them it's a 'news release' or 'news from' at the top.

Newsrooms are busy sometimes to the point of looking frantic to the untrained eye. Unless you've visited a newsroom or talked to people who work there you'll have no real idea of how busy they are. If you haven't been, go. If you take a daily paper, you are talking about a team of people producing the equivalent of a short novel every day. That's not an easy task. What's more, it's a book that is interesting to read, that takes account of how the reader likes to receive it and is well-written. That means that it needs to be focused, time-driven and organized. Many authorities would benefit from a closer examination of the media organization and systems in their area.

So, if you don't tell them it's a news release they won't know it is one. And when it shuttles into the office along with thousands of other bits of paper, you will give them one more reason to bin it.

It should say what your organization is

Apart from the obvious convention of saying who you are, which is always a good idea in any business context, making it clear that the release is from a reliable, credible source makes it more attractive. Remember, you are an important source of local news. Surprisingly, though, many local authority departments use their news releases as a way of asserting their independence. So you will see releases from 'the department of leisure development management' or even from some unit within the authority. Such subtleties are wasted on the local media. In fact, by signalling the differences in your council you do two things: first, you confuse them – they might not be sure it's from the council; and second, you tell them that your departmental identity is more important than your council identity. If the news is from the council tell them and if you do happen to run the 'Procuring Services For The Year 2010 Unit', keep it to yourself.

Make it look established

How many of us would have faith in our bank if every time we got a letter the letter heading was different? It's a sure-fire way of getting your customers to take their money elsewhere. It does not signal 'reliability, confidence and established'. By the same token, if you are trying to send out a 'reliable' message, maintaining the form is one crucial way of doing so.

Again, in any one authority you will find many different press release formats. Why? If you want to give the impression that you know what you're doing you should have one format and stick to it. That way, when your release comes down the line the people receiving it will know what it is. You won't surprise them. They will learn to mentally recognize reliable news as it comes in and as for hand-written press releases, if you want to get an incompetent message across quickly take out a small advertisement in the local paper.

It should be dated – with today's date

How long would you continue to read a newspaper if it constantly fed you out-of-date news? Not long. Since the news media have to establish their credibility, too, they need to churn out news not history. You, as an organization selling them news, need to show them that your news is timely, hence the date. They will make a judgement on that basis but since they won't have a special pigeon-hole in the office for your news, it will get judged alongside everything else that comes in. And it's all judged on the basis of is it relevant, newsworthy, etc today?

Some people leave dates off convinced that the timelessness of their story will somehow come across. Again, it's part of the form which if omitted sends out the wrong signal.

It should have a clear headline which encapsulates the story

The purpose of the headline is to get the story across as quickly as possible. Don't try to make it a clever *Sun*-type headline but rather boil your story down to its essential facts. Headlines are written by sub-editors in newspapers. They are highly unlikely to use your version. It's there primarily to say to the journalist 'This is important – read it'.

For example, if you are sending out a press release saying that your council is about to introduce productivity-related pay as part of 'best value', don't dress it up.

This headline is interesting:

'Council to introduce productivity pay deal for staff'.

This is not:

'Best value arrangements may mean introduction of productivity-related remuneration package for certain staff'.

Both may be true but the latter sounds boring and introspective – something written in language you understand and speak rather than that spoken and understood by the recipient.

The first paragraph should tell the story and answer five key questions and they are:

116

- who?,
- what?,
- where?,
- when?, and
- why?

You can add a sixth, how? In a fuller form these questions become: what has happened?, who has it happened to?, when did it happen?, why did it happen? and where did it happen? It shouldn't surprise you that this is the convention. After all, when we read or listen to the news those are the questions that we want the answers to. If a man was killed trying to rescue a cat from a roof we want to know who he was. We want to know that it happened today and we want to know where he lived. If you live in Southampton and it happened in Scotland you won't be interested. Similarly, you will be more interested if there are 'why?' reasons which make the story different.

Sometimes officers find it difficult to use this first paragraph convention. Because of the culture of putting in the background, or in committee reports, the recommendations, the news paragraph is often put in later. There have been draft news releases circulated where the news doesn't feature in the release at all but is saved for the notes to editors. If you make it too difficult for the journalist to find the news, they won't and your release will quickly find its way into the bin.

The first paragraph is not easy to write. So you shouldn't worry if it takes a while but if you remain focused on the essential facts it will be easier. Here are some examples:

A council leader today said that staff must increase productivity by 10 per cent in return for job security.

Dampshire Council is to introduce a new bye-law banning drinking in Dampley town centre.

Subsequent paragraphs should add facts and opinions to the story

Once you've told the essential facts, you then add in additional details. If you've said in the first paragraph 'a council leader' you could add in 'councillor Joe Smith said …' You would also want to add in where he said what he said and perhaps some indication of why. You could add a brief quotation which would give the paragraph additional weight.

It should quote key players – people who have a legitimate contribution to make

Quote only those people who have a legitimate comment to make. Remember that the press release should be constructing its own credibility in the same way as other communications. So think: what do you need to add to make the piece believable? A council press release will typically include a quotation from a council chairperson or a senior officer. Try to avoid the 'council spokesperson' speaking. Unless your organization has a tradition of using a spokesperson for all major announcements, and is, therefore, able to accumulate credibility it could be seen as a cop-out. If someone has a legitimate comment to make let it come from that person.

Quotes should be written as though they have been spoken

When a quotation, which originated in a press release, appears in print it should look as though it was spoken. The reading public will not register that this was not actually said. So if it reads as though it was written it is less likely to be covered. For a fuller analysis of sound bites see below.

However, as a general point people do not usually open sentences with the likes of 'notwithstanding' or 'following extensive consultation and involvement processes'. Remember the audience. They want to know that you're speaking to them.

It should be typed, double-spaced or a space-and-a-half

This is a convention which is for the benefit of the journalist. Once a journalist has decided that they will use a particular press release they are likely to sub-edit it. They may want to change the order of the paragraphs. They may want to delete words or sentences or add in additional quotes. That will be possible if they can write between the lines. If your press release is single-spaced it is very difficult to do that.

It should be on one or two sides of A4 paper

If you recognize and register with the media that you know they have very little space they are more likely to carry your story. You may feel that your story merits seven pages but unless you are talking about the state of the nation and your release is from Buckingham Palace on the eve of the Queen's abdication, forget it. Space in the media is related to their perception of importance. The more space, the more important. It should follow, then, that you keep your releases relatively short.

Technical detail or explanatory remarks should be saved for the 'notes to editors' which follow the main release

Clarity can all too often be lost in a press release by including explanatory remarks or background detail. It is important from time to time to include detail. You may want to include legislative references or fuller explanations. Put these in the 'notes to editors' at the end of the release.

When it is ended it should say 'ends'

This is another helpful convention. In a busy newsroom, where there are thousands of pieces of paper floating around, you need to tell the recipient that they have all of the pages which have been faxed. And if you put 'ends' when you have ended then they will know that they've got the lot.

It should give a phone number where you can be reached and if you may be reached out of hours, where you can be contacted

It's surprising how frequently people leave this out or put a daytime number only. Remember you are trying to sell your story to the media. You're asking them to use up their space for your ends so make it as easy as possible. If you send out a press release at 4 pm, which you would like to be used on the morning radio show, make sure they can reach you in case they need further information or clarification.

Briefing the media

If you want to put the trading relationship on a more formal footing you can use media briefings. It is possible to create locally the sorts of media relationship which exist in the lobby system nationally. It is a matter of 'institutionalizing' the relationship you have with the media and formalizing the terms on which you pass on information.

It would be possible to set up a regular contact with local journalists where they get access to key decision-makers and policy-makers. In return for such exclusive, advance access, journalists would give the council coverage, but it openly breaks with the spirit of open government, as it tends to be described, because journalists could be given access to the news before it goes to committee.

How would it work?

First, you would have to establish that local journalists were interested in regular access to key people – the leader, chief executive, other senior councillors and managers. Next, you would need to clarify with both parties what the boundaries and rules were in relation to how such meetings were reported. Finally, you would have to agree, in outline, how journalists would view these meetings. It would be important to reach an agreement on how information gleaned through this source would be reported. In the end, the arrangement would only work if it was in your mutual interest. It might be that you would have one section which was on the record and another part which was off.

There should be no shortage of material. Every decision which went before the ruling group could then go into a press briefing. It would help combat one of the biggest challenges to local government management – leaks and chairpersons briefing against each other.

Press conferences

Press conferences are expensive and risky events. It's best to reserve them for occasions when you want to address a number of media at once, where you don't need to differentiate your message for different audiences and where you believe that journalists will be attracted to the event. If there was a major emergency where there was a great deal of media interest a press conference would be one way of managing media interest.

A press or news conference gives an organization an opportunity to present the news from their point of view. It should be a planned event which tells the media:

- what the story is;
- why it's important – if that's not self-evident;
- who the key players are;
- what their position is.

Ideally, if you were thinking of running a press conference you would give journalists sufficient notice to make sure they've got the best chance of getting there. You would tell them what it is about, why it's important and who will be there.

How do they work?

Since you are effectively, in the same manner as a press release, preprocessing the news, you will need to establish your reasons for holding a press conference – know why you're holding one. The following are some basic points to consider.

What is the essential story?

Remember that journalists are busy and if you drag them out of the office for an hour (it would appear to be difficult to make anything shorter than an hour in local government) they will need to have the story presented to them.

Normally, you would use the first part of the press conference to tell journalists why you've called the event. You would explain what the story is and you would introduce the other parties, if there were any, to journalists. You would then provide an opportunity for journalists to question the other participants. It will be important to manage the questioning process, ensuring that all journalists have the opportunity to question those fronting the event.

If there is more than one party involved (such as police and the local authority) it will be important to meet before the conference starts and to decide who will say what as well as where the points of agreement and disagreement are. It will also be important to determine how long the event should be. This will be a question of balancing your needs to be sufficiently fulsome with the journalists' need to meet deadlines.

But be clear. What do you hope to get out of holding a press conference – in the context of a press release, an interview, or a media briefing – as ways of getting the message across? What will this approach give you that the others won't?

Will the venue support your essential message?

If there has been a major emergency and you want to indicate that you are calm, concerned and in control make sure that the venue says that. If you've got people rushing around and there are constant interruptions your 'in control' message would be likely to suffer.

Will the speakers know what they're going to say?

Strangely, people organize press conferences as opportunities for journalists to ask questions without first deciding what they want to say. It's a bit like going into an interview without knowing what you want only magnified and if you are not used to dealing with the media you might find yourself saying things you'd rather not.

If there are different agencies (you might involve police and the health authority alongside social services in a health story) do you know what your common ground is? This is about recognizing that you probably don't agree on everything but it's better to know that in advance. It's important in areas where there has been loss of life. The media will often want to know who is to blame. It may be that one organization wants to use the press conference to allow the blame to fall on one set of shoulders. Pre-meetings allow you an insight into how your 'partners' will play the event but it's best to know in advance rather than find out you are to be 'stitched up' in the full glare of publicity.

Do you know what you don't agree on and know how you are going to deal with questions in that area?

It's worth teasing out alongside the actual story what the various areas of interest are. You can also agree who will lead on what and how you will handle the questions which cross over. It's best to have a simple line to deal with discomfort.

Have you thought of the kinds of question which will be asked and what you will say when they are?

The best way of looking at this is to decide what kind of headlines could be written about the story. Imagine you are a customer or a client and you've just found out what's going on, what questions would you want answered? Don't forget that although journalists will be polite in asking difficult questions, they will also be persistent in seeking out the answers and that may mean going to other places in your organization to find them.

How long is it going to last and how will you divide up the time?

Quite simply, you need to recognize that journalists are busy and you will, therefore, need to give them the news as quickly as possible and create time for questions. If the story is a running issue, such as a disaster which is actually happening, you may want to arrange subsequent press conferences throughout the duration to keep them informed. If your conferences are timed to help journalists meet their deadlines then you are more likely to retain their interest.

In the final analysis press conferences are one of the tools which can be used to get your message across. However, it is essential that you think through in advance how you will gain or what you will lose by adopting one media route as opposed to another.

Photo opportunities

These can be a way of getting easy coverage. Newspapers and television like image-driven news. Try to think of your story in terms of pictures. Think of how the last government tried to persuade us that eating beef, for example, was safe. There was a picture of the minister with his child eating a beefburger. That single image said so much more than endless words about the crisis to that point. When you put photo opportunities together try to think about the audience you are trying to reach and what kinds of images will be important to them – the beefburger image, because it was put on during the main evening news, which has a high proportion of family viewers. Children in the audience would have been able to relate to the minister's child as a peer. Parents in the audience would have been able to relate to the minister as a fellow parent and as such the single image was a powerful way of effectively reaching several audiences simply and simultaneously.

The media can be a very effective way of talking to local people. It's worth remembering that, given the public nature of local government business, they will be interested in reporting your news whether you like it or not. That means that if you are to get the best out of your news you will need to manage it proactively. At the same time, given the importance of local newspapers to local people, the way that you do so must at all times help forge a strong relationship with the local media. It's likely that the local newspaper editor will be more believed than the council leader. The only axe that the former will have to grind will be the need to sell papers. With the council leader, though, life is more complicated than that.

7 Mind the gaps – putting together a communication strategy

In this chapter I will look at communication strategies and how to use them. In the last decade there has been an increasing emphasis on authorities having communication strategies. Whether they are designed to involve local people in decision-making around policy initiatives or whether it is about informing local people what the authority has done for them in the preceding 12 months, organized communication is a vital element. However, there is little point in simply saying that the authority should have a communication strategy unless it is somehow linked to management action. In short, officers and members from an authority need to be saying and *acting* in concert and they need to be listening to what local people (or whoever the audiences are) are saying.

However, strategies can be complex beasts or worse still they can be simply a set of words on paper. This chapter examines them as a series of gaps that may arise between the strategy and reality and explains how these gaps need to be crossed if communication is to be an effective means of achieving management outcomes. As such the chapter focuses on a number of separate elements:

- the definition gap;
- the objectives gap;
- the achievement gap;
- the reality gap;
- the credibility gap;
- the action gap;
- the resources gap;
- the measurement gap;
- the power gap.

I will then go on to look at communication currency. I will suggest that there are models that we all use to explain the way that people behave in our society and that we each need to understand them if we are to be able use communication effectively. We argue that these models underpin the common sense that we all rely on to make sense of the world.

COMMUNICATION STRATEGIES

Local authorities are filled to the brim with communication strategies which are no more than tomes and are best left on the shelf. That is rarely the fault of the author, often a communication specialist, who has put it together. On occasions these strategies have been created by PR professionals with very little discussion with the rest of the organization. It is critical before any strategy is created that some key questions are answered. Often, though, these questions are not asked by senior managers of themselves. The result is that the strategy which is created does nothing to advance management action.

This section identifies the following nine gaps which need to be crossed in order to create a communication strategy:

The definition gap

When you are putting together a communication strategy you must be clear about what you are trying to achieve. So far as the strategy is concerned this is getting managers to accept the definition of communication management. In other words, the management of the form, content and context of information in order to bring about specific outcomes. By starting at that point they will not think of the strategy as the press releases that the PRO should send out during the course of the exercise. Equally, managers will think of the strategy as external communication. However, if you are sending *out* messages that conflict with the messages that you send *in* them, the inconsistency which inevitably results will undermine your strategy. Critically, it is wise to define a communication strategy as the sum total of all management action towards a specific outcome.

The objectives gap

Here lies the problem: with most strategies the outcomes are too non-specific. Any strategy will need a clear definition of objectives. What specifically do you want to achieve? The hurdle here is clarity. It is easy to say 'We want to create an enabling authority'. The strategy will happily promote that idea and you may even have various opinion-formers wandering around the community armed with that mantra but what does it mean? It's not that it is indefinable. Rarely, though, do managers (or for that matter politicians) take it any further than that.

For example, there are a number of ways of defining the enabling authority. Who are you enabling? What are you enabling them to do? What if you enable them to do things you don't want them to do, what will you do about that? If you are trying to create an 'enabling climate', what does that mean? If it means getting people to feel that they can express their own ideas in management action so long as it meets the needs of the community, that might be a good starting point but then you open up a number of other definition areas. What is meant by management action? Which community are we talking about and so on?

The central problem is not the concept of the enabling authority. It could equally apply to the concept of empowerment, facilitation and 'best value'. In the absence of a clear definition of goals, it is unlikely that any communication strategy will deliver your objectives.

Clarity is the key. If you define your objectives in terms which are measurable then you will know whether you have succeeded or failed. So an objective might be that we want 20 per cent of local people to express the view that Blankshire District Council is doing a good job. That is measurable but inevitably it raises another question – how well are you doing now? A crucial part of defining objectives is the gathering of reliable information on a regular basis.

A key part of defining the objectives in your strategy should be setting a baseline. Once you know where you have started you are more likely to be able to plot a realistic course forward but, more importantly, communication does not exist in a vacuum. *Other management action will need to be taken in order to achieve the objectives*. That will need to be scheduled. Those taking the action will need to know what else is being done. It may sound blindingly obvious but you will often find the organization saying one thing while doing the opposite. For example, your authority might decide to promote itself as the enabling authority to external audiences. However, unless your internal messages say the same thing and *do* the same thing, your staff will not own the message and may well wander the corridors maligning any claim you make publicly. And like all objectives they are meaningless unless you define time-scales, lead officers and so on.

The achievement gap

This can also be known as the rhetoric gap. How many places in the UK are currently proclaiming themselves as 24-hour cities or towns? A fair few and yet, if you were to wander the streets at 4 am you might struggle to find a burger bar open. It's easy to make these claims but the recipients of such claims are not daft. If there is too great a gap between claim and actuality you will simply undermine the validity of your communication. What's more, you will blight the credibility of other comments your organization makes.

This is about aiming at a realistic target. Of course, it's not the catchiest thing to say, 'Blankshire – moving slowly beyond mediocrity'. No one would want to hear that but if actual outcomes and communication are to relate to each other in any real sense, you will need to define your achievements in real terms. Evidence matters. Ask difficult questions of yourself. What are we achieving now? How much can we expect to achieve one year on? What other priorities might we have? What other pressures? Is there any evidence, on the basis of what you know about previous management action, that you will achieve what you are claiming you will?

In the election campaign of 1997, the Labour Party deliberately reduced expectations to a number of specific achievements. Since their election the new Labour Government have been very good at setting out specific desired and low achievements. By keeping expectations low and making deliverable promises, each claim enhances their communication rather than the opposite.

The reality gap

Take stock. If you are using a communication strategy to change perceptions you must first set a baseline. It is vital to find out how are you seen at the moment. To achieve this, one way of doing it is to conduct a survey. You don't have to have the expertise in-house. Local authorities already use organizations such as MORI or the British Market Research Bureau could put together a survey to test whatever perceptions you want to measure.

This will provide you with information about the reality you are dealing with. If, for example, you establish that your council is not deemed to be credible by the people you are hoping to work with, you will have to solve that problem before you can proceed. Look, for example, at the demands put upon local authorities to establish partnerships with various stakeholders. It is likely that you would put together a strategy to position the council with these various stakeholders. You might want to send out messages about being open to the ideas of others, keen to exchange ideas and to take joint management action.

How, though, do your stakeholders see you at the moment? Local businesses may simply feel that your red-tape approach gets in the way of everything they try to do. Different communities may see you in different ways. Some may believe that you do a lot for them. Others might feel, perhaps because of the politics of their area, that you do nothing. Schools, another key partner, might still feel aggrieved because of the way you handled the opting-out issue some years before. You can't simply start with a blank sheet and ignore all of these perceptions. You need to take account of your starting point with each audience before you plan future action. It may mean having to meet with different audiences in different ways in order to move each into the same new position.

So never let reality out of the room. Warm, feel-good statements might appease senior managers and politicians, though unless they're connected to the real world you might as well whistle 'Dixie' and read the paper.

The credibility gap

Once you have a grasp of how you are seen it's time to take stock of your credibility. We discuss this further in a later chapter but it is important that you understand the nature of your credibility. How many unfulfilled promises have you made or how many are you making? This is made more complex simply by virtue of the size of your organization. In essence, you may see your council as different departments and units but the public may only see one body. Leisure services and housing are just the council. When you are putting the strategy together it must, therefore, be built from a position where you can see the whole picture.

Performance indicators may give you the first part of that picture – you will know how well you are doing in each of the service areas – but you will also know how well you have promised to do. What, for example, did your politicians say about last year's performance? Did they promise to sort out the time taken to process planning applications, for example, and have you done it?

Other essential sources of information are comments, compliments and complaints. What is the nature of these? These will let you know not only who is complaining (and, therefore, who you might target) but also why they are complaining and how they are complaining (which will give you clues about what language and means you might use to respond to them). Again, before you start proclaiming the *new* in your strategy, you will want to know how many of the problems associated with the old you will first have to solve.

There is a second credibility gap which concerns the originator of the communication strategy. Like any high-profile product there is a danger in making promises which you either don't keep or can't keep. Often public relations staff are asked to deliver undeliverable things – 'We want to get a good press always.' Spot such hostages to fortune in advance and deal with them. Unfulfilled promises kill careers. It's about being clear about what you can and cannot achieve.

The action gap

This is the absolutely crucial gap to fill. If you really want your strategy to sit and spend its life on the shelves of people's offices, then action doesn't really matter. If, however, you want your strategy to affect things, then its vital to make sure that there are a real set of actions that flow from it. What will you actually do and when? What specific messages will you send out, to whom and when? What action would you expect them to take as a result? This requires a systematic, planned approach. To fill the action gap you will need to identify:

Audiences

Who are you trying to reach?, what social groups do they belong to?, what symbols are important to them?, what languages do they speak? and in what ways is it spoken (vocabulary, style, etc)?

Media

This is the means by which you reach your audiences. You should know as much as possible about the media. Radio stations, for example, will know which audiences listen to their programmes at different times of the day. Newspapers will have reasonably reliable data on their readers. There are niche publications which will reach virtually any interest you can imagine. Details of these can be found in publications such as *Benn's Media Guide* but knowing the audience and getting coverage for your message are entirely different things. You will need to think about how you shape your message for the medium you are using.

However, the media does not only refer to publications or productions. In essence, the meaning of the medium should be consistent with the message that you are sending out. It may be, for example, that you are seeking to position your chief officers with the business community. It may be the first stage in putting together partnership arrangements. It would be unlikely that you would want to broadcast this through the local radio station. In seeking to create those vital first steps you would probably use a medium which they might be familiar with. It should also be a medium which holds a particular meaning for the target audience.

Key messages

These are the phrases that will be repeated to your target audience. They must support your key objectives. So far as your audiences are concerned your messages are what they consume. If you repeat endless vague and meaningless statements then that will be what they will read. At the same time, in hoping to get your messages covered, you will need to take account of the needs of the media, but be clear: you are sending out key messages in order to achieve a specific outcome. If you are saying: *Blankshire – tough on vagrants, tough on the causes of vagrancy*, over time you would expect people to believe that *but only* if that is how it appears on the streets of Blankshire.

One way of ensuring that your messages have impact in whatever medium you choose to use is to create sound-bites. One of the main reasons for creating sound-bites is the limited space which is available in virtually any medium to transmit your message. If you are trying to get your point across, for example, in a regional television interview you will have no more that 10 to 12 seconds, or roughly 30 words. If you are talking to a newspaper they might afford you a paragraph (between 20 and 35 words) but even if a local BBC radio station, which can offer a two to five minute interview, gives you air time your audience will not have unlimited attention. If you are speaking on a breakfast show, consider the number of pressures crowding out your words in the audience's minds and you will appreciate how important encapsulating your message in a few words is. It will not surprise you that you can use the same techniques in letters.

There are a variety of techniques you can use to package your messages into straightforward messages. These have come to be known as sound-bites.

1. Three-part lists

If you can break down what you want to say into three parts then it will be more memorable than either two or three. For example: 'I have nothing to offer you but blood, sweat and tears.' It's usually possible to find ways of turning your ideas into three parts. If in doubt consult a *Thesaurus* and find different ways of saying the same thing in synonyms.

2. Claim and explain

This is about making a claim about something and following that by an explanation. For example, 'If we don't stop driving we'll drive ourselves in to an early grave. Pollution on British roads is worse inside the car than it is outside'. What you give is the message encapsulated into a simple chunk. Of course, you could go into endless explanations but the longer you go on the more audience attention you could lose.

3. Contrasting pairs

This is about saying what something is by reminding people what it's not. Again, it helps encapsulate your essential message. For example, 'This section is not about teaching you ways of communicating; it's about teaching you ways of communicating effectively.'

4. Repetition

This is a rhetorical device which helps your audience build links between segments of what you are saying. It helps to establish themes and it helps to create expectations about what will come next. Predictability helps comfort audiences, for example:

… remembering on both sides that civility is not a sign of weakness, and sincerity is always subject to proof. *Let both sides* explore what problems unite us instead of belaboring those problems which divide us. *Let both sides*, for the first time, formulate serious and precise problems for the inspection and control of arms. *Let both sides* seek to invoke the wonders of science instead of its terrors.

(John F Kennedy, 20 January 1961, A new generation of Americans).

5. Alliteration

Using words which begin with the same sound makes them more interesting to listen to even, surprisingly, when more meaningful words might have been substituted. For example, 'This document is about how we pull people together to maximize our potential' as opposed to 'This document is about how we bring our staff together to maximize our resource.'

6. Metaphor

Complex ideas can be easily conveyed using metaphors. Imagine you were trying to get across the idea that a local authority is a collection of different departments which, although working to a common agenda, have independent and autonomous control and management systems. You could say that 'Blankshire District Council is a flotilla of ships all moving together towards one destination.'

7. Simile

The same applies to a simile, saying what something is like. It allows you to get complex messages across quickly. For example, 'Poor bureaucracy is like knitting fish.' It is critical that your choice of simile also conveys the meaning that you wish to convey. It is possible to think of all sorts of striking similes but which would be inappropriate given the audience?

8. Rapport

It is important to bear in mind the emphasis that a group of people (or individuals) can place on particular words. When you are talking to or writing for an audience think of the words they would want to hear or read.

Focus on the outcome

In the context of managed communication, it is important to use words for a purpose. Crucially, you must be conscious of that before uttering them. If you are trying to impress your audience you may use one set of words but if you are trying to appear friendly and warm the same set of words may not work.

Remember feelings

It is worth putting this in a separate category. Think before you create your sound-bite how you want the recipient to feel once they have received it. Write it down. There are a wide range of possible human emotions: love, anger, hate, envy, motivation and guilt. Which do you want to create?

Don't overrun or expect endless patience

Remember that unless you are the Prime Minister you won't be able to expect people to listen all day. Check out the reaction: did you succeed in your objective? Did your sound-bite work? It's easy to come up with words but since words should be outcome-driven you need to ensure that you get the outcome you want.

The resources gap

For your strategy to happen you must carry out as realistically as possible a quantity survey of the work ahead. A communication strategy, if it is real, will eat up resources – money, time and energy. You need to know that those resources are at your disposal. If they are not, find out whether you can get them. Cost out precisely what it will take to implement the strategy. It may also be that there are particular skills you will need to make the strategy happen. It's surprising how many senior managers will take on communication jobs that they are ill-qualified to do. Somehow, it seems that everyone is a PR expert. We don't apply the same standards to other professions. If we were to visit casualty we would be staggered if the janitor decided to take a blood sample. If you don't have the skills and expertise find someone who has. In every local authority there are a limited number of managers who really enjoy developing new ideas and practices. These developmental managers are vital resources for carrying out your strategy. Other managers may find anything to do with PR bewildering and a bit scary so make sure that you obtain some of the time of the developmental manager.

The measurement gap

How will you know whether your strategy is working unless you define its success in measurable terms? The more specific you are about what you are trying to achieve the better the chance of measuring whether you have come up to the mark. There are many established means of measuring communication activities. It could be simply adding up the following crude measures:

- the number of column inches;
- positive versus negative coverage;
- what it would have cost in advertising space;
- the number of repetitions of your key messages.

However, since strategies are concerned with outcomes it will be better to measure outcomes in the same terms. For example, your communication strategy may be supporting an inward investment strategy. You might, therefore, be concerned with:

- the number of visitors to the area;
- the number of relocation enquiries;
- the number of relocations;
- the views of those who have relocated.

There is one other set of measures which you will need to build into your strategy. In the process of nurturing opinion-formers and allies you may have led them to believe that there was something in it for them. Make sure that when you define success you do so *in their terms*. Remember that this is a foray into the credibility marketplace and your own stock can go down as well as up.

The power gap

A key feature of whether you are able to achieve anything in a political environment is weighing up whether you are able to muster support for your project. This is no less the case with communication strategies. An effective corporate communication strategy will pervade many elements of the way people do things in your council and before you change things you need support. Those who will benefit from the change – for example, those putting forward the public face of your message – may be very keen but others may be less so. What's more, you may find that there are moves to block your actions.

For a middle manager to be effective in carrying out a communication strategy, you must put it into the political context of the organization.

Allies

When you are putting together your communication strategy take account of the people you can rely upon to help you. What opinion-formers are on your side? These are people others will look to in order that they can decide what to think about a given subject. Newspapers are often opinion-formers. In a council, chief officers and leading members will be opinion-formers but in any management situation there will be those whose ideas are taken seriously by others. You will need to know who they are and whether they are on your side in which case they could be allies. If they are not allies you may need to originate a separate strategy to win their support.

How do you do this? Work out why anyone would want to support what you are doing by looking for what may be in it for them. What is their agenda? What do they want? You may, for example, carry out a motive audit on your key opinion-formers.

Motive audit

This is simply working out what drives each of the people who you might be seeking to persuade to be allies in your communication strategy. It is not an easy thing to do. If you simply say to people 'What do you want to achieve?', they are unlikely to tell you straight out but they will give you clues in their actions. Also, you can find out through third parties who may be close to them. If you want to know what the council leader wants, befriend his or her PA. Get close and understand what drives them. Look at what the opinion-former does. What meetings do they speak at? What causes do they appear to support? Check out their history. How and why did they get to where they are today? Once you know what people want it is easier to make a judgement as to whether or not you can help them get it.

For example, you may be putting together a communication strategy to promote partnership working. Not everyone will be keen – it takes up time, it means working in new ways and it may mean the possibility of exposing managers to unfamiliar working practices. However, a senior councillor may be motivated by the possibility of high-profile work by being seen to be leading-edge and so on. They may also be a former businessperson. You could engineer it so that this councillor is leading the thinking on partnership working. They would have credibility in the marketplace and, as a leading councillor, they would be able to convey seriousness, something which would be helpful in promoting partnership working.

Enemies

It is safe to assume that whatever you want to do, there will be those who don't want it to happen. Assume that the status quo will always benefit a number of people. Think about who they would be. Now, think about what impact your communication strategy will have on the status quo. Who will the winners and losers be?

For example, you might be putting together a strategy promoting Blankshire as a happening authority. Such an approach is attractive until you start to consider the questions around it:

- When did you become happening?
- Why now?
- Why did you not happen before?

In the course of those questions some people may be singled out for attention by the media and others. We are all prisoners of our past. So, think about how potential enemies will behave (and specifically what they would do) should your communication strategy be successful and expose them as failing in some way.

Of course, knowing this danger exists, some might opt for non-threatening strategies. This can be helpful in not making enemies but should you be forced into woolly thinking then you might wonder whether it is worth bothering about in the first place. Alternatively, knowing that potential enemies might emerge you could develop a strategy for turning potential enemies into allies.

COMMUNICATION STRATEGY IN ACTION

The following is a case study of the way in which one council organized its messages in order to achieve a better working relationship with its business community during the period of the Local Government Review.

Case study: 'Local government is our business', by Robert Underwood, Barrister at Law, former leader of North West Leicestershire District Council

During the local government review in 1992, North West Leicestershire District Council was keen to win the support of a number of different interests in the locality. The Local Government Commission had made it clear that they wanted to see tangible support from the community. Until that point, although we could demonstrate support from our traditional community, we rarely had ownership in the business sector and yet it was important.

We put together a strategy for gaining that support which took account of how we were seen and how we thought they would want to be seen. Rather than inviting members of the business community into the council chamber to meet us, which would be perceived as our territory, we decided to meet them in their familiar surroundings. Businesspeople, we thought, would be attracted by the idea of a business breakfast.

We thought it should take place at a hotel normally used for business, but which wouldn't be perceived to be extravagant in terms of council taxpayers' money. It took place early in the morning. Because we didn't want to interfere with our guests' working day and because we were keen to signal our business focus we started at 7 am and we set out to create an atmosphere which said to them 'We feel comfortable with your approach'.

Every aspect, from the slogan (local government is our business) through to the specific words used in the leading speeches (choice, liberty, bottom line, etc) were all chosen to show that we literally spoke their language.

We arranged tables to allow our officers to respond to and engage local businesspeople. The speeches were short and to the point. We talked about how our case would help their interests. The whole event was about showing that, contrary to popular opinion, local government 'could hack it'.

The result was the beginning of a stronger relationship with the business community which persists to this day. Not only did we win their support for our bid to the Local Government Commission but we also began a useful dialogue with a powerful and influential stakeholder group.

What this example demonstrates is the importance of developing a strategy to meet the needs of a particular audience. One of the biggest challenges facing those who would put together communication strategies is overcoming the need to have one strategy. Local authorities are complex organizations. There are many things happening with different audiences simultaneously. It can be tempting to think that you can get the whole council on-message. Achieving that, particularly when you consider that it is the sum total of all individual transactions with publics that ultimately determine how people feel about you, is next to impossible. Of course, you can get staff to parrot 'We are a listening council' or some other nonsense, but again if the message has no integrity – because while you may hear you rarely listen – then they might as well recite the Bangkok telephone directory.

Critically, we can all manage our communication. It is important for councils to determine what outcomes they want to achieve and those will be best achieved through a combination of managed communication and management action. In the end, the effective combination of those will deliver real results and help overcome the many cynicism barriers which exist inside and outside local government.

8 Shape your future

In this chapter I will consider ways in which organized communication can help address some of the crucial corporate issues which face local government at the turn of the millennium. If local government is to be an industry which engages and involves its customers then their officers need to be aware of the impact that each of them personally has on that mission. One thing is clear. There are more opportunities every day for individual members of staff to affect perceptions of their authority than those presented by the media.

The media are interested in very few of these interactions. A local authority manager who wants to use all of these different possibilities has to realize that every interaction with the public must be used to provide the wider message of a customer friendly service. Stories in the media are a very small but very important part of this process. The local authority that leaves that to the PR managers alone will fail to get its message across. What's more, in each interaction with a member of the public, managers have the chance to understand their customers needs in ways which can never be possible through one-way communication.

This chapter is not just about identifying the issues related to communication. Instead, it demonstrates how managers can use communication to further some of the main policy themes that concern new local government. In each section we outline some ways of approaching the development in local government by using better communication. The solution to ineffective communication is to find ways of improving it.

Ultimately, that must be a matter for each member of staff. In our everyday lives, when we make an effort to take communication seriously, the result is higher-quality relationships. Taking the trouble to really communicate pays enormous dividends in our personal life, but just as it's impossible to legislate for that in our personal lives so, too, would such an approach at work prove unworkable. In our professional activities some officers will certainly fail in the same way as many of us do not meet the needs of our friends and families.

The series that this book is a part of identifies a number of structural changes that are taking place in the world that local government serves. These themes of modernization for local government and its relationship with the wider society require managers and staff to consider their place in the community and the ways in which they can meet their community's needs. Any organization which depends for its very existence upon contributions made via taxation is likely to be under scrutiny. Where that organization is open to public inspection, as local government is, it can expect to have its judgements questioned from time to time. Where it is deemed deficient by the media and others it can expect to have to justify its existence, its decisions and its services. However, while few other sectors of public life will be the subject of so much microscopic inspection, equally few will have the reach into the community which local government enjoys. That advantage puts a local authority in a unique place, that is, to be able to shape perceptions of itself and the community in which it is located.

We also look closely at the following developments in new local government and show how better managed communication can improve them:

- working with a modern workforce to communicate the message;
- creating and maintaining the local authority – the meaning of a corporate image;
- engaging the local community;
- the importance of locality for local media and local authorities.

WORKING WITH A MODERN WORKFORCE TO COMMUNICATE THE MESSAGE

Modern local authorities will need to develop an involved and active workforce. They can only achieve this if they recognize that the workforce both collectively and as individuals are a major form of communication with their local public. Strangely, the importance of staff in council communications is often ignored. You no doubt have seen instances when a council will be promoting itself to the community as a listening organization at the same time as it is failing to listen to the people who work there. While that might be the way that industrial relations need to be conducted from time to time it creates a potential contradiction which undermines the message sent out.

Staff, particularly lower-paid staff, tend to live in the local area and when you consider that local government is in many parts of the country the biggest employer, there may be a great many people in the community telling it like it is. In an earlier part of the book we talked about the need to engage staff and to help them become ambassadors for the authority. Where this is not done staff will actively talk their employer down. If this came from customers it would be damaging enough but when it comes from the people who should know best, those who work for the local authority, it can be very damaging.

Of course, there is nervousness among staff. Some will be loathe to admit they even work for a local authority. Tired of images of council workers being characterized as lazy and useless in the media, some councils have taken a 'get tough' line on relations with staff. The attitude that they ought to be glad they've got a job is not uncommon and while no one would question that staff need to be effective and customer-focused, berating them will not help achieve that. Any communication strategy which fails to take account of the way that staff will behave, and how they might describe their experiences at the council, will be doomed to almost certain failure.

We have heard the phrase 'Our staff are our ambassadors' but have never seen the full recognition of this label being given by a local authority. One campaign I designed for a council involved members of staff putting a sticker on their rear car windscreen but few were prepared to take part. It was later discovered that there was a sense of not wishing to be identified with the local council outside work. It is difficult to know whether that feeling is widespread among the 2.3 million people who work in local government but if it is it's not surprising that local government has a bad press. Because we tend to believe the people who work in organizations more than the literature they pump out, one poor comment from an aggrieved worker will go a long way to damaging the public image of an authority, especially as this image is multiplied through the staff member's family. Multiply that by up to 15 000 in some authorities (as much as 40 000 in the biggest) and you have a substantial image problem on your hands.

There is no easy answer to this problem. Staff relations are complex. Quite apart from normal industrial relations, authorities are having to embrace 'best value'. The next few years will be very challenging. There are moves away from producer-led decision-making in councils where authorities consider services in terms of their own needs.

The most advanced authorities have moved well beyond traditional municipal thinking and are working with partners to provide the services that local people want. As authorities look to other provider solutions there may well be contraction. Local education authorities, for example, have already seen this happen since the introduction of the 1988 Education Act. Professional education officers, once a thriving breed, are now an endangered species.

However, alongside this, one thing is very clear – the quality of the services provided, the leadership in an area and the image of the council itself will depend upon the nature of staff relationships within that authority. It will no longer be enough for councils to say that they value their staff unless they actually do. That is why there are two chapters in this book dealing with issues of communication internal to the local authority.

It will be vital that the techniques which authorities are beginning to apply to their local communities, those of engaging them and winning their support, are also applied to the people who work in the sector. Of course, it will be possible to continue to run authorities with staff who are grateful to have a job. The unemployment queue is still sufficiently long for that threat to keep most people to heel but what a wasted opportunity. An employee who feels under threat will not thrive and neither will they proclaim the qualities of the authority to every soul they meet. If local government is going to be a dynamic, involving, leading beast then it will only be because the people who work there are and that means the rank and file. There is a limit to what the policy-makers and the strategists can achieve. Sooner or later you have to start doing something. It will be those who do, for they interact daily with customers, who will ultimately make the difference.

Every member of staff in every local authority can have a profound influence on the perceptions others hold of their council. We know from our own experience that one individual can shape the way that we feel about any organization. Some organizations understand the importance of personal communication as a means of managing perceptions. Anyone who has taken their children (or themselves) to McDonald's will be aware of the ways in which staff are trained to present themselves to you in a way that takes account of your needs. That's because McDonald's understand that if you manage perceptions from the minute you walk in until you walk out with your Big Mac five minutes later, then you will add to the overall impression that your customer has of your organization. That experience will, if it is managed well, continue to build customer loyalty. This will lead to revisits and this, in turn, will lead to a healthy profit. McDonald's realize that all the advertising in the world will be undone if an individual member of staff is rude, so they make sure they are not.

CREATING AND MAINTAINING THE LOCAL AUTHORITY – THE MEANING OF A CORPORATE IMAGE

As a middle manager you will not be concerned with the creation of a corporate identity for your organization but you might be tempted to create one for your unit or section. This is not unknown, particularly among independent thinking units. But you would be strongly advised against this.

Local authorities, if they are to survive at all, must be able to project a strong identity as an organization. One of the main strains in local government is the tension caused by individual departments that follow their own ends and their own image. Each department that depends on following its own ends has the potential of tearing the local authority apart. It is, therefore, important that the corporate authority has some power to construct its own role and meaning. This section is designed to assist middle managers in understanding why corporate identity, if it is to be used effectively by local government, needs to be centrally controlled and carefully managed.

To many the corporate identity of an organization is the logo that sits at the top right-hand part of letters sent out to customers. Or it might just be the rather grand version that sits above the reception desk or in the heart of the council chamber in your council. The problem for corporate identity is that this is only the tip of the conceptual iceberg. If corporate identity is identity then that must mean more than the symbol that encapsulates or communicates your organization.

Corporate identity is as much behaviour and dress as it is image. In that sense, the identity or logo itself is nothing unless it reinforces the culture and approach of the organization. The following section will help readers understand why it is important to resist the temptation to 'improve' or 'customize' existing council corporate identities. It is also designed to help understand the ways in which middle managers can help their staff change their behaviour to reflect the corporate identity.

Know what you are

Before creating a corporate identity for an organization it is important to consider what it is. Just as our clothes as individuals should reflect how we see ourselves as well as how others see us, so an organization's identity should do the same. However, the problem is that it is often difficult for the people who work for an organization to say what kind of organization it is and it's not just that we are too close. It's as much to do with the fact that we tend to fall into clichés too readily and say what we think others might want to hear. Ask any group of middle managers questions about what organization they work for and you will hear the contents of their mission statement verbatim.

One approach to the question of identity is to look at the question through a different set of eyes. For example, you might want to ask if this council was a car what kind of a car would it be? You could equally ask what kind of animal it might be. In examining your answers it would be important to consider why you think what you think. That will tell you more about how you (and your staff) really see yourselves.

Know what others think you are

It is one thing for Blankshire Council to see itself as a dynamic, thrusting organization. The people of Blankshire may not see things in the same way at all. You need to know what they think about you and why. And, crucially, what elements of you, as a council, cause them to see you as they do. For example, they might think that you are dynamic and thrusting when you answer the phone because you always answer within three rings and because your policy is not to pass customers from pillar to post. However, they might believe the opposite of you when they arrive at your public counter only to find your reception staff overworked and distracted.

Know what you want to be

This is about being realistic. If you are 'a safe pair of hands' council and you want to be seen to be ahead of the wave and dynamic, then you'll have to change more than your logo if you are going to convince anyone that this might be the case. Underneath any move towards repositioning your organization there will have to be some hard-nosed management thinking. If you accept that identity needs to be made real in terms of staff action, staff attitude and behaviour, the organization will have to consider whether this is realistic, but it is important. Not only will your new logo be meaningless unless it is communicated through dress and behaviour, you will be roundly criticized for wasting money on squiggly lines.

Involve your stakeholders in defining your new reality

When you are defining what kind of organization you want to be you will need the support and involvement of everyone who will make that identity real on a daily basis. It's easy, childishly simple, to produce a new logo for an organization but people worry less about logos than they do about behaviour. Customers are more likely to remember poor telephone service than they are to remember that you have a two-coloured fish at the front door.

What you are doing in creating or redefining a corporate identity is making a statement about corporate behaviour. In essence, you are defining the nature of the reality that will be experienced in your organization. Others will already have a view about the reality of Blankshire District Council. Those people will be your staff and your customers. Each group is a stakeholder. And if you want them to disinvest in your current *reality* – which may be there by design or by default – you will need to engage and involve them before selling them the new reality. Fail to do this and all you will have, in practical terms, are a series of complaints wandering around your corridors.

Define all manifestations of your reality

Corporate identity is an opportunity to encapsulate a defining moment between you and your stakeholders. Through proper involvement you will be able to establish what your staff and customers expect from your council. Isolate those aspects and use them to build agreements on ways of acting and behaving. Used effectively you will have the beginning of a contract between you, your staff and your customers. If your organization is positioning itself, through its identity, as a caring, involving organization, then you will need to think about how that sits alongside all of the other behaviours staff and stakeholders will associate with your council. For example:

- How will you answer the phone?
- How will you deal with customer complaints?
- How will you approach staff involvement and development?

The list would be longer than this book. The point is simple: if you reduce corporate identity to the shape of your logo then you will be ignoring the very things that give you your own identity. When we shop in McDonald's we learn to associate the 'M' with all of the behaviours that make up a successful eating experience and McDonald's know this. They will want us to associate the 'M' with cleanliness, low cost, high-quality food, served by committed staff quickly, efficiently and effectively. Their approach is consistent – whether you go to McDonald's in Moscow or Manchester – the experience will be broadly the same. Can you say that the meaning of your corporate identity is either as clear or as consistent?

Think about what the corporate identity will look like

This is the least important aspect of corporate identity. It is the easiest to put together. Resist the temptation to create a competition for local schoolchildren. As a rule it's better to use professionals to undertake this kind of work. You will either have an in-house team or an outside agency. It will be important to involve stakeholders in the choice of the final design. It should mean what you mean and once chosen you should develop a manual to indicate how it should be used. Like all identities, if you change it (by virtue of not having the right size, colour or placing) every five minutes then it will have the same impact as changing the way we look frequently. Some may enjoy looking at the fashion parade – others will simply think you don't know what you are.

ENGAGING THE LOCAL COMMUNITY

One of the biggest challenges facing local government in the next 10 years will be involving the public in local democracy. Part of this will be the need to involve communities in the decision-making process. That work is already underway in a number of councils with different degrees of success. Added to that middle managers and members alike will need to get close to partners who will assist in meeting community needs.

It would be easy to underestimate the difficulty that local government will face in trying to meet these challenges. With a culture which is broadly introspective and where there is little movement between the public and private sectors, there is a danger that senior officers will not be able to build those vital links with outsiders.

And there is a need. In May 1998 the local election results resulted in turnouts below 30 per cent up and down the country. This could cause communities to question whether the local council has a mandate at all and perhaps it is a testimony to their lack of engagement that they rarely ask the question. Public perceptions of local authorities are poor. In a survey conducted by MORI in 1997 it was established that local councils lag well behind other public utilities in terms of providing information about their services. BT and British Gas are market leaders in keeping people informed.

However, it's not just about providing information. That will be important, but local democracy, though, is about so much more. Local government will need to engage and involve local people if councils are to have any chance of achieving the desires laid out by the Prime Minister, Tony Blair, in 'Leading the way'.

The way ahead will not require massive expenditure. While vast public poster campaigns could cause local people to sit up and notice the council, it's quite likely that they would result in negative coverage and, therefore, be counter-productive given that services are stretched because of poor funding. If local government simply used glossy posters to get their message across, with no thought for the reality of their services on the ground, local people would soon find their council wanting. That, in itself, would damage the authority's credibility. It's far more important that staff and members are able to engage the people they deal with.

For a local authority to be part of the new millennium it must find ways not only of involving people, but of taking that message to the core of their business. Communication and its use is a key part of that process. The following section includes some pointers on ways of involving local people in council business.

Make it clear that there is a benefit

Each of us is driven by the need to know *what is in it for us*. We all know that local elections are poorly turned out but where is the information campaign which makes it clear what the benefits of voting are? Yes, there are lots of messages about 'losing your voice' but if you have a voice that is rarely heard and even where it is it makes no difference then you might as well stay mute.

First, though, be clear: are there any benefits? It's all very well to trot out all the democracy routine but what does it really mean to most people? Reduce the electoral system to its roots and you have less than five minutes of your life standing in a wooden cabin with, as Paul Corrigan puts it, 'a stubby pencil'. Unless you make it clear what the benefits are to each potential voter of going through this thoroughly unpleasant Victorian experience then there won't be much change in voting patterns.

The same applies to involving local people in decision-making. Councils are mad on consultation. Finding out what people want is fine – if they tell you. However, in order to get local people fully engaged you need to be able to demonstrate that there is a direct benefit to them in return for their investment in a process which they, broadly, will not feel comfortable with and may not fully understand.

Explain your failures

There won't be a council in the country that has delivered all of its promises but we wonder how many will have explained why not. We suggest that there will only be a few, if any, who have apologized for not delivering, for making a promise, involving and consulting people and not fulfilling those promises. Is it any surprise then that communities are loathe to invest anew?

Councils, like individuals, trade in the credibility marketplace. If you make a promise and don't deliver, your stock will fall and if you consistently fail to explain yourself, you will lose all credibility. And what will happen is what already happens – people simply don't get involved.

Design processes for involving people which start from the point of view of the customer

It's easy to consult if you always consult on your own terms and on your own territory. It's also a sure-fire way of keeping people away. It's important to ask people how they want to be consulted. Do they want you to go and talk to them at weekends, in the supermarket, in the evenings, via phone-ins, through the local newspaper or radio station? If you are going to get people to give up their time give them a return. Convenience is one way of making it easier to involve.

Another way is to pay people. Market research companies pay people to attend market-testing sessions. Why don't councils do the same?

Keep people appraised about progress

There's nothing worse than being asked for a view on something and then never hearing anything more about it. We all like progress updates. Local people and potential partners are no different. Before you start the process of consulting and involving think through how you will keep people in touch. It may be that you use your council newspaper. You might think of putting out leaflets in targeted mail-drops. You might be able to persuade the local media to carry your message. On running events like consultation that might be difficult. It's not a sexy story to say 'We're still thinking about it'.

Don't bore people

How many of us would give up an evening of *EastEnders* or *ER* to go and watch six saggy grey suits sit behind a table in a musty school hall? It's hardly passion-rousing stuff. If you are going to engage people you need to know what they like. Controversy will get people out on a damp night. Anyone who has tried to close a school will know that this will fill hall after hall but it's not the kind of approach you would take if you were trying to promote a forward-looking, engaging authority.

There is a move towards citizens' juries and customer panels and these can be powerful ways of engaging a small number of citizens in the decision-making process. But a different approach will need to be applied to the mass market.

It's important to learn from others. Look at the most successful retail stores – Virgin, M&S and Boots. Look at how they get people in. Bright colours, engaging artwork, a well-trained sales staff. It's critical to remember that the way that officers behave inside the council will be interpreted differently outside. So change the way you behave to take account of the needs of local citizens.

Look at the experience from the point of view of those you want to involve. Does it feel threatening? If so, make it less so. Does it intimidate? If so, change it. Does it look boring, or uninvolving or vague? If so, unless you change all of these things then numbers will stay low.

Use little things to demonstrate that you are listening

Councils have opportunities to demonstrate that they are prepared to listen to people virtually every week. Think of planning applications. Councils are obliged to publish details of planning applications but look at how most are published. They are often small, poky adverts stuffed into the back of newspapers where they are less likely to be found. It is difficult to find many which would engage you in any way at all. They are also difficult to understand as the language can be very technical. Everything about them says 'Don't pay attention to me'.

Now it is probably convenient not to have planning applications plastered across the front page of the council's newspaper but, of course, that's what happens to them. Controversial applications will be picked up by the local press and then the council will find itself in a defensive position.

Think for a moment about how that looks to local people. The council was, in the first instance, in control of the information and has the wherewithal to publish it. They choose to do so in a way which makes it as apparently difficult as possible to understand. That doesn't look like the listening council in action. After the story blows up in the press it's likely that local people will be more inclined to thank the paper for bringing up what would otherwise have slipped through unnoticed.

If a council wants to be seen to be a listening organization then it must listen all of the time. Listening sometimes, particularly when it suits the council and no one else, is not listening at all. We all know from our own experience that if someone only listens when it suits them then that is self-interest by another means.

Rather than having all-encompassing listening strategies councils would do better to think as the people who live in their area think. Involving people wherever possible is more likely to result in being perceived as an involving organization.

Avoid political expediency

It can be politically expedient to get people involved, or to appear to, when you are about to do something very unpopular. It can mean that your process is watertight from the point of view of anyone who might question decisions afterwards but doing so also means trading on trust.

It's important that there are benefits in getting involved. To what extent, for example, might you actually take on what people say to you and change your plans altogether?

Involving the public in local government is hard. Both the public and local government have got out of the habit of working with each other and reacquaintance will be hard. However, if local government wants a future there is simply no alternative to finding how in your local authority, with your service, you can provide that reconnection. When you try and fail the first thing that is likely to happen is blaming the public for not being interested in you. However, the problem is they are the only public that you have got and getting them interested is your problem and not theirs, so if you give up on them it is you that will suffer not them. You can never elect a new public – you are stuck with the one you have got and making the relationship work is initially your problem.

THE IMPORTANCE OF LOCALITY FOR LOCAL MEDIA AND LOCAL AUTHORITIES

One of the core meanings for the industry of local government is the importance of locality. If the public felt there was nothing special about their locality, then there could never be anything special about their local government and the whole point of different democratic government in the different localities would disappear. Therefore, a local authority needs to foster people's experience of locality as much as possible.

Interestingly, local newspapers also have to foster a sense of locality. If the South Blogtown *News* wants to be different from the North Blogtown *Gazette,* then the residents of South Blogtown need to feel they are different from the residents of North Blogtown, otherwise they might as well just have one newspaper or one local authority with the same news on both. And we all know how undesirable that would be.

For most local authorities local newspapers are the most important means of reaching local people. While most journalists who work in local papers have never worked in the public sector, they belong to a different world but they still belong to one that believes in locality.

When this book was first put together, we considered it important for readers to see life in a council through the eyes of a senior journalist. I asked Peter Mitchell, a former news editor with the *Coventry Evening Telegraph*, to give his perspective on how he, as the person who daily determined how the council would be seen by the community, saw councils. What he wrote was an analysis of the way in which local media need to keep in touch with the pride and prejudices of local people about their locality.

Pride and prejudice

Local newspapers act on strict codes. There's the Press Complaints Commission code of conduct which acts as a sop to those who wish newspapers to be ruled by law. There's a code of commerce which means large loyal advertisers get preferential treatment. There's a code of content which governs what appears on news, features and sports pages. This is the code you have to crack if you want to exploit a newspaper to your advantage.

The code is made up from pieces of pride and prejudice. The following lists the items covering local government:

■ People are proud of the family they come from, the street they come from and the town they come from. They are proud of the town's football team – even though it is at the bottom of Division Three with the worst defensive record in Western Europe.

- They are proud of local industries – even though the giant chemical works pour out daily doses of toxins. They are proud of their town's place in history – even if this is limited to the fact that Britain's most notorious sex killer lived there, the country's worst train disaster happened just up the track or that the landlord of the Spotted Calf in Birch Street once played drums with Showaddywaddy.
- They are proud of past achievements but believe that they will never be matched either in the present or in the future. They believe their home town is undervalued by a prejudiced outside world which has never had its eyes open to the real Rotherham or hidden Hartlepool.
- They themselves are prejudiced against rival towns – especially those within a 30 mile radius of home. They believe rival towns cheat on the football pitch and have been given more central government aid, more industrial and cultural grants through, at worst, corrupt favouritism or, at best, sharp practice. They believe that their town's lack of inward investment, unemployment, poor housing and education, dismal High Street shops and night-life, dog mess on the pavement and declining civic pride is the fault of their local council.
- Even though they have husbands, wives, uncles, nephews and neighbours who work for the local authority, all council workers are overpaid, overprotected, underworked and underachievers. None of them would survive in the 'real' commercial world but none of them will have to because they have jobs for life.
- Councillors are even worse than council workers. They are only in it because they are career busybodies who fancy a free trip to a twin town once a year and they are on the take from every property developer in the region.

The code made up from this list of pride and prejudice is ingrained in the culture which local newspapers claim represents their readers' interests. Some of the code's characteristics are also internal characteristics of the local newspaper. When pressed, many local newspapers also believe that their own past achievements and particularly the number of readers they attract are greater than those of the present day or of the future. They will only admit this in private. In public, they will tell you of their efforts to diversify into new media.

Local newspapers serve up the diet of pride and prejudice from front page to back page in every edition. On a typical day, a tour of editorial content will encounter news stories detailing the planning committee's latest failure to stop intrusion of the green belt, a leader article condemning that failure, an industry page campaign to generate more pride in the successes of local firms, a letters page littered with complaints about dog mess, street lighting and the lack of public conveniences, a memories column about the good old days when the town's gas works employed 400 and a biased back page match report which skates over defensive failings and blames the referee.

Each ingredient of the code of conduct supports another. It means that publication of an editorial leader supporting a local planning decision is as likely as a football match report slagging off the home team. The code has remained constant for many years. Its guardians are 40-something sub-editors, letters page compilers and long-in-the-tooth municipal reporters who pass on their expertise and experience to each generation of itchy footed young reporters as they pass through on route to temporary freelance shifts on the *Evening Standard* or the *Daily Mail*. The career structure produces mature national newspaper reporters who consider all stories about local government to be beneath them and unworthy of attention unless they involve the exposure of corruption on a mass scale.

Those who wish to manipulate local newspapers, using them to convey the right message in the right way to the right reader, must use the code of conduct in its entirety – both positive and negative. The trick is to smother the unpalatable prejudices with a liberal dose of pride. For example, faced with the delicate task of informing local families that a waste incineration unit is to be built near their homes, also state that it's 20 times cleaner and more efficient than the latest built in a neighbouring town, that it will provide 50 new jobs on what was, after all, the site of a famous wartime munitions factory and that you intend to name it after a famous footballer but would like them to help you choose one.

The need for local councils and local newspapers to follow the same rules of engagement has never been greater. In the age of competitive tendering, at a time when one council is set against another in the tournament to gain central government aid, towns and cities succeed by presenting a united front. Applications must come with public consultation and consent. The easiest way for councils to acquire proof of public involvement is through the window-dressing of local newspapers, self-proclaimed people's champions.

In recent years, this new need has resulted in the creation of partnerships between local councils and newspapers in a way that, previously, would have been impossible to envisage. These partnerships are founded on and draw strength from local pride. However, beneath the surface, old prejudices still exist. Newspapers still regard themselves as watchdogs of grass roots democracy acting as the unofficial opposition in communities dominated by one political party. At the same time, newspapers drawn into these new relationships find it impossible to criticize honest attempts to improve local conditions, however far-fetched or misguided they might seem.

Local government often hands the job of dealing with local newspapers to people who do not know the code of content, are unwilling to learn it and, in the most stubborn cases, do not accept that it exists. A false sense of human enlightenment or political correctness means that they neither accept the pieces of pride nor the points of prejudice. These people are known as press or public relations officers. PC PR (politically correct public relations) is perhaps the single most hated enemy of local newspaper journalists. Those who persist in its practice are doomed to failure.

Yet, the important way in which the local media works to reinforce and recreate local people's relationship to their locality contains a lot of important lessons for local authorities who also have to foster this relationship. Obviously there will be clashes between local government and local media about how the local authority is viewed, but both need local people to believe in the specialness of their locality. Because of this local authorities and local media have something in common which a wise local authority manager works on all the time.

CONCLUSIONS

Ultimately, neither staff nor members should expect the communication which takes place between them and local people to be easy. Neither should the communication which takes place within a council. Communication, if it is meaningful, is rarely easy partly because it is the means by which different individuals realize their goals. Inevitably, not everyone can be happy. One person's planning permission is a blot on the landscape at the front door of another and inevitably, when resources are squeezed and cuts fall, someone has to explain why it happened. The messenger is rarely welcome.

However, it is through such dialogue that mutual understanding grows. Uncomfortable communication is still communication. Worst of all is not the unpleasantness which surrounds the democratic process, it is the indifference. When people do not care enough to walk a few hundred yards to vote once every four years then democratically founded bodies have got real problems. As the mandate bleeds away so does the security of that institution. Communication is no less crucial inside authorities. If staff believe that all communication is top-down propaganda then they will be less engaged employees. Trust will not grow and when given the chance to comment on their employer they may be less than charitable. Only a fool would suggest that these problems are easily surmountable but since local government is one of the most important parts of British life only a fool would fail to try.

9 Making sense of communication

This final chapter attempts to give readers another perspective on communication. It will argue that it's not simply about getting information across. Rather, we communicate because we want something to happen, we want an outcome. It begins by looking at definitions of PR starting with what might be described as the industry standard definition. However, as with all definitions there are difficulties in terms of everyday practice of PR and we examine those briefly. The chapter then moves on to look at the concept of communication management and discusses how middle managers can use the concept. The chapter ends up by considering the ways that notions of common sense run through our communication and the implications we all face as a result.

Everyone in Britain is involved in public relations. Each of us makes decisions every day about the way we speak, act and communicate in order to get what we want. The main difference between professional PR people and everyone else comes down to skills, awareness and repeated application but we can all learn those skills. Anyone with children will have learnt that they know that there are ways to get what you want. These skills are learnt early and stay with us for life. This book attempts to reawaken your communication potential and apply it to your work of managing in the new local government.

PR is part of the way local government works. At its most obvious a local authority that has no relations with its public has become divorced from it. Local authorities are spending more time than ever involving their communities in decision-making. That means talking their language. However, since we are all communicators and since all middle managers in local government serve the public, PR is much too important to be left to the PR professionals. This book is intended to help middle managers harness the management of their communication so that they can realize management goals through effective PR thinking. As such this is both a book for PR practitioners and effective managers. Wherever possible I have tried to use examples which might typically face managers in their day-to-day work.

DEFINITIONS OF PR

First, I will look at some definitions of PR. The Institute of Public Relations, the professional body to which many PR people belong, have a clear definition of public relations: 'PR practice is the planned and sustained effort to establish and maintain goodwill and mutual understanding between an organization and its publics'.

So far as non-PR managers are concerned it is probably of little use but it is worth examining the definition and teasing out some points which may be useful. There are a number of positives in the statement:

- It is endorsed as the benchmark for the profession. The IPR is the recognized and respected body which is pushing this particular definition. In any field of knowledge it is critical that a shared understanding of what you are supposed to be doing is developed. In that way PR people can be seen to be one of the professions which make up the senior managers in local government. Perhaps, surprisingly, IPR membership is not thought to be vital in applications for senior jobs.
- There is a stress on relationships with the public rather than relationships with the media. One of the crosses that public relations has had to bear is that it is seen to be press relations. In that sense it is seen to be the art of getting your picture in the paper and while many PR people do spend time, sometimes a substantial proportion of their time, managing media relations, this emphasis divorces PR from management results. Rarely will management outcomes be solely concerned with how something will look in the media. It is more likely that managers will be concerned about what will happen as a result of what appears in the media. The stress on relationships is important.
- The definition also recognizes the interactive nature of PR. Like all communication, it is about sending and receiving. And, crucially, it is about the way in which the sending can be reshaped, to make it more effective, directly as a result of the feedback received.
- Finally, this definition highlights at least two outcomes which should come about as a result of good PR – goodwill and mutual understanding.

There are a number of negatives:

- The definition fails to make clear why an organization should want to maintain goodwill and mutual understanding. While few would argue that these are not in themselves good things, it might equally be argued that since goodwill and mutual understanding will cost resources to establish, there should be a purpose in doing so. At the same time, there may be periods

when the absence of mutual understanding, for example, could be beneficial in management terms. In negotiations, where one party is seeking to
gain advantage, a lack of clarity might help that party to advance their position.

■ This approach suffers from the motherhood and apple pie syndrome. It's
'all things to all people feel' means that it might lose credibility. Not only
will different PR people behave in different ways but for reasons mentioned earlier it will probably be desirable for them to do so.

■ Neither does the definition explicitly accept that specific results, other than
goodwill and mutual understanding, are possible without goodwill and mutual understanding, making it tautological.

■ Finally, it says nothing explicitly about internal communication and culture
and, without doubt, if an organization is to communicate effectively with its
external publics it must first do so effectively with its own staff. So far as culture is concerned the definition says nothing about the way that communication takes place and what impact that will have on behaviour,
expectations and so on.

Frank Jefkins, a leading writer on PR, sought to take the definition further on:
'PR consists of all forms of planned communication, outwards and inwards,
between an organization and its publics for the purpose of achieving specific
communication objectives concerning mutual understanding'. Again, there
are a number of positives.

■ This definition goes further than the IPR and recognizes the actual role of
a PR practitioner as someone who may be concerned with both internal
and external communication.

■ It also recognizes the link between communication and outcomes. Although he believes these outcomes should result in mutual understanding,
nonetheless that action-reaction connection is established.

■ Finally, it recognizes the breadth of PR activity.

On the negative side:

■ There may be too much of an emphasis on planned communication. This
could equally apply to the IPR definition but the reality of day-to-day-life
depends upon knowing what you're trying to achieve and then achieving it
by whatever means. That may mean planning, and in the best of circumstances you would plan every detail, but it will also mean being opportunis-
tic – using any set of circumstances to your advantage.

■ Equally, when applied to business circumstances, clients are probably
more likely to be interested in results, usually measured in profits, than
in mutual understanding. If a PR agency is employed to make potential

customers aware of the benefits of using Luxo soap powder, for instance, it doesn't really matter whether they are able to understand the organization selling it. What will matter will be whether they buy it.

- Jefkins' definition shares the IPR's concern with positioning the profession rather than helping the profession understand what it is about. In any profession, particularly one which is relatively immature (the IPR celebrated its 50th anniversary last year), part of the job of practitioners is to help solidify the body of knowledge which constitutes that profession. If the profession is to survive the ravages of misunderstanding and misinterpretation, then it is vital that all members of the profession are able to articulate what they do.
- Finally, it does not recognize the specific part played (where that is appropriate) by PR practitioners within their organization in the overall tasks undertaken by that body. What is missing is the recognition that PR is a tool which, to be effective, must act in concert with other management tools in order to bring about specific outcomes.

The final definition we look at is that put forward by the Mexican world assembly of PR practitioners. It says: 'PR is the art and social science of analysing trends, realising their consequences, counselling organisation leaders and implementing planned programmes of action which will serve both the organisation and the public interest'.

The positives:

- It recognizes the bigger picture. There is a clear relationship between PR and strategic business outcomes.
- It also recognizes the role of PR practitioners as advisers. In many organizations they will be in a coterie of people who will advise senior managers on action and, in that sense, working alongside other management advisers such as finance, personnel and legal, they will seek to help an organization realize its business goals.
- It also recognizes the role of PR people as individuals who have influence in a managerial environment, and certainly if public relations is to be a management tool it needs to be located close to decision-makers if it is to have an impact.

On the negative side:

- This definition does not define its terms. That it is both an art and a social science allows it to be everything without ever stating what it is to anyone.
- The definition works independently of the concept of the public interest. It suggests that somehow the ways in which messages are managed and the

public interest are entirely separate. While that will be the case in some industries, manufacturers of beans will rarely concern themselves with the public interest save on grounds of health and safety, that is not the case when you look at government information managers. PR professionals in the Central Office of Information or in the Government lobby will be very much concerned with shaping how the public sees matters.

- Further, this definition makes little or no distinction between the interest of one public as distinct from those of others. Different publics have different needs, different languages and different expectations. None of this is recognized.

- Finally, there is a failure to recognize the situational problems associated with advising and counselling within an organizational setting. The definition rightly focuses on the activity rather than the individual concerned. However, whether that activity is recognized as PR when it is carried out, sometimes inadvertently by others, may be another matter.

However, as far as most managers are concerned, how PR is defined by others is irrelevant. What matters is what it means in terms of what managers do on a day-to-day basis. The next section looks at the concept of communication management and how to use it.

COMMUNICATION MANAGEMENT

Here we look at how communication can be used to help bring about specific outcomes. In that sense, although this approach characterizes how PR people tend to operate it is also the way that we all behave every day of the week. You may, for example, want your children to spend a bit more time reading and a lot less time watching television. Persuading children to do anything is incredibly difficult, but you might well focus on how you can persuade them to use what they are reading to help them achieve the things they themselves want. If you are very clever and don't like television yourself you might package watching television as 'boring', an ever present word in the vocabulary of young people.

The concept of communication management put simply is this: it is the management of the form, content and context of information in order to bring about specific outcomes. Each of the three elements – form, content and context – are crucial.

Form

Form refers to the shape of what you are saying. The shape of your communication, the way you put your language together in terms of sentences, specific words and so on, will have a strong influence on how it is received.

You can change the shape of any communication and achieve different outcomes. Take a simple example:

I am writing to inform you of our decision on your benefit.

As opposed to:

This letter will inform the recipient of a benefit decision.

Broadly, both sentences say the same thing. The first is more personal, because it addresses the subject as 'you' and refers to the writer as 'I'. The second is less personal. Where the concept of communication management differs from the idea of writing in plain English, it is precisely because there may be times when you, as a manager, may want to achieve a less personal effect in your writing.

Content

The second element in the concept of communication management is content. When we communicate with someone we make decisions about the content that we believe they should receive. That decision will be conditioned, probably subconsciously most of the time, by a number of questions:

- What do they need to know?
- Why I am telling them this in the first place?
- How much do they need to know in order to understand what I am saying?
- How much do they need to know in order to do what I want them to do?

You could simply be telling someone something because you want to transmit information, but rarely, in a management context, are you simply sending out signals. Usually, there is more to it than that. When we send out information we usually want to achieve something. There is a motive. For example:

- I am telling this person this because I need to be seen to be communicating.
- I am telling this person this because they've asked for the information.
- I am telling this person this because if I don't I'm storing up problems for myself later.

When you select information, the choice and the ordering of that information will be governed by a set of complex questions. Where managers are less aware of the power of communication, the questions and motives that govern the selection of information may not be the same questions and motives which govern the decision on form. It is through using both the form and content consciously and consistently together that you are more likely to achieve the specific outcome you are desiring.

Say, for example, a colleague enquired about the work you were undertaking on a new project. You might want to share information with them in a way which made it clear that you wanted a closer working relationship. You might say:

> I've been thinking about your interest in our best value work and I thought we might spend a bit of time working on some of the ideas together.

However, if you wanted to make it clear that you wanted to retain or even extend the distance between you, you might take a different line:

> I can now respond to your interest in the best value work and I thought a meeting could be appropriate.

Of course, it's not an exact science. Different words will have different meanings for all sorts of reasons, and we discuss that later, but the examples serve to illustrate the point that form and content are powerful elements in the management of communication.

Context

The third element of the definition, the context, is less manageable. The context refers to the place where communication happens. Place refers to everything from the room, the space between two individuals, right through to the historical moment, the political context and so on. You might list context as:

- space – the physical place where something takes place;
- time;
- culture;
- country;
- power relationships between individuals;
- current social trends;
- history of the relationship to this point;
- what the individuals know of each other.

Most of the context is outside our control but if we are aware of it we can take it into account when we communicate. You will have heard it said that politics is all about timing. That comment refers to that specific element of the context. Communication management is about being aware of the impact of the context upon what we might communicate. The same sentence uttered in different contexts could have a completely different outcome.

One place to examine each of the elements of communication management is in the area of personal discomfort. It is when people feel awkward or uncomfortable in social contexts that you will see bad communication management in place. Some people find the informal moments that surround formal occasions very stressful. For example, if you have to give a report to a committee and you are asked by your boss to attend a small reception for committee members just before the committee meeting, the context for communicating the information to members of the committee will have changed. You will have prepared to communicate in a formal setting and may find getting the same matter across in an informal one very hard indeed. The content may be the same, but the context will be very different. If you fail to appreciate this you might appear foolish, talking to people over a cup of tea as you would to a formal committee.

However, communication management is not just about managing words and utterances. What we do in any given set of circumstances can say a lot. Indeed, it is the actions which we take in any situation that can so often have a real and lasting impact on those we communicate with.

ACTIONS SPEAK

The above section has emphasized the importance of words in managing communication. In a previous chapter we focused on the way that symbols are managed in order to bring about outcomes. Equally, actions, during which no word may be uttered, can speak volumes.

This exercise is designed to get you to think of the different outcomes which may arise from changing either the form, the content or the context in a given situation.

 Exercise: embarrassing moments

Part one

Think of an occasion when you felt deeply embarrassed because you said the wrong thing to the wrong person in the wrong place. First, write down what you said. Next, write down how you said it. What was your tone of voice? Comment on the space you left between your words, say something on why you chose the words you did and so on. Then write down where you said it. What kind of occasion was it? Who was there? Try to get down as much detail as you can.

Finally, write down the essence of what made it an embarrassing moment. What was the single factor that really made you blush?

For example:

I remember when I said, 'Where's your idiot manager today' without realizing that he was just behind me. I said it in the Chief Executive's office. And I said it the week after my one to one with her when she had commented on my poor interpersonal skills.

It was embarrassing because it made it look as though I hadn't listened to a word she'd said.

Part two

Now, group the situation into three distinct areas:

■ the form of what you said;
■ the content of what you said;
■ the context within which you said it.

And in a separate column write the word 'outcome'.

You might find that you are unable to separate form from content. So if something appears in two columns that's OK for the time being. Now change one element of the embarrassing moment and see what impact it had on the overall outcome.

For example:

I remember when I said, 'Where's your idiot manager today' without realizing that he was just behind me. But this time, it wasn't said in the Chief Executive's office.

Think about this for a moment, try to feel how it might have felt and then write in a separate column the outcome.

Do the same thing with each of the elements of your situation. In the end, you should have a list of different outcomes. If you find that you always have the same outcome you will either need to dig deeper into the elements of the embarrassing moment or, if your crime is too dire, give yourself over to the police.

MANAGING COMMUNICATION AND MANAGEMENT

In an earlier section one definition of public relations was about managing information to bring about specific outcomes. In that sense it shares a strong base with management which might be defined as the management of resources to bring about specific outcomes.

In working terms, then, public relations would be used to help bring about the goals of the organization, or part of the organization, however defined.

Crucially, though, PR activity is already part of management action.

When a manager asks a member of staff to carry out a specific action they will already use PR thinking to achieve that. They will define the task in a way that is easy to understand. The instruction will be phrased to achieve maximum cooperation. The instruction will take account of the situation or context. The language will be designed to take account of the needs of the particular individual. The member of staff will be given the opportunity to say whether they have understood the instruction.

Arguably, every manager who communicates the task that they expect their staff to carry out is a PR practitioner. Managers will usually have to think about the way in which their staff's actions will communicate a message to the public, so they will also have to think about PR in that sense, too. However, it is the application of PR thinking as a deliberate act which differentiates what might be called good management from active PR. Crucially, managing the new local government demands that managers are active and that they actively manage how their part of the organization communicates within itself to the rest of the organization and to the public. It concerns being conscious of the ways in which changing each of the variables elicits a different result.

If we are to use communication as a tool, as a means of achieving particular outcomes, it is important to recognize some of the assumptions which sit beneath our everyday communication. A lot of our communication, particularly that used in an everyday sense in a council, relies on shorthand to be effective. We share assumptions about what particular words mean and we share assumptions about ways of behaving which are indicated by particular forms of communication. Furthermore, when we relate to the media it is worth bearing in mind that they, too, hold assumptions about the world.

The final part of this chapter looks speculatively at the notion that our everyday communication is rooted in common sense. It will explore some of the models which we all use to explain how people behave and which give sense to our communication.

COMMON SENSE AS COMMUNICATION CURRENCY

Common sense is the context within which we understand our world. It is not universal. All cultures have common sense. This will be what is considered right and wrong. Of course, there may be some universal truths such as those relating to human rights which permeate all common senses but the common sense which contextualizes what we do will be delineated by the way we do things here. That 'here' may be in our office, in our authority or wherever. The easiest way of understanding its influence is to think what do the people we are communicating with need to understand in order that it makes sense in the way we intend.

Broadly, common sense is not written down anywhere and yet it is central to our day-to-day understanding of the world. It is the taken for grantedness of our everyday life. Common sense enables us to determine what actions mean in our society. It is something learnt from the day we are born but it is also a shifting body of meanings.

By referring to common sense we will know the way that other people will perceive our actions. For example, nowadays in local government, if a manager decides to tell a racist joke at a staff meeting it is likely that this will cause offence. This common understanding reflects changes which have gone on in our society in the last few years. We must all be sensitive to changes in common sense and we are. Because we know how important these ways of behaving are we will be able to adjust our actions almost immediately. We would know, for example, that while a joke about the Princess of Wales' love life would have raised a wry smile before her death, afterwards it would have been grossly offensive to most people. Even today it would have to be told in very select circumstances.

However, common sense does not exist in a vacuum. It is the accumulation of bodies of knowledge which are shared and reinforced through a variety of key sources. These sources will include the proclamations of key individuals and opinion-formers (world leaders, politicians, intellectuals, the media and so on).

We focus on two overall parts of common sense. If common sense is to be used as part of the repositioning process, then it will be important to understand the ways in which it works. First, we look at some of the models at work within common sense. Second, we focus on the myths or stories which pervade common sense. These are ways of explaining how people behave and the means by which we might predict which way they may behave.

Models

Models help us make sense of the world. They are constructs which enable us to predict the way that things will happen and how people will behave in certain circumstances. The idea here is that we will apply these models to others' behaviour as a means of understanding what they are doing.

The market model

The rules of economics, of supply and demand, not only determine the way that our capital exchanges work, they also underpin our understanding of day-to-day life. We will expect, for example, that the more exclusive something is, the more desirable it will be (supply and demand). We will also know that if you are doing something, the more you keep on doing it the less you will get out of it for every successive unit of effort (the law of diminishing returns). And we also know that if we are to make something seem exclusive we must attach additional meaning to it.

Blame must find a home

In the blame culture, when something goes wrong there must be someone to blame. It is as though it is possible to apportion blame on the basis of outcome. Our legal system is rooted in this kind of thinking. Juries, when hearing a case, will be looking out for the person that they can blame the crime on. Defence barristers, recognizing that their client may have committed the offence, will be seeking to attribute reasons for an individual's actions. There may be extenuating circumstances. This concept reinforces the idea of blame.

Cause and effect

Essentially Newtonian thinking – all actions have equal and opposite reactions. In behavioural terms, actions have consequences. This helps reinforce the concept of blame. If something happens we will look for reasons and although we do accept that bad things do happen, there will still be an implicit view that there will be contributory factors. In essence, cause and effect is a simplifying construct which enables us to make sense of the world quickly. Following the death of the Princess of Wales, we immediately looked for a cause. The press photographers were lined up as the most likely culprits but as the weeks moved on and more evidence became available, they simply moved from the being the cause to being contributory factors.

Heroes and villains

A very powerful construct which underpins story narrative in popular culture. This element is reinforced on a daily basis. Virtually every soap opera will use this. The Hollywood film industry relies on this approach. In any given story (whether it is our own story or one we are consuming) there will be a hero fighting for what is right and villains who are trying to prevent this. It will look as though evil will dominate, right up until the final frame, but in the end good will triumph over all. Western spiritual thinking is rooted in this – God (and Jesus) as good, Satan as the villain.

Innocence and youth

We have a belief that when we are young we are innocent of all evils and that it is life that pollutes us. It is perhaps because we so believe in this idea that we are shocked by tales of crimes that are carried out by young people. The James Bulger case illustrates this point.

You are what you are

This is enshrined in the phrase 'a leopard can't change its spots'. It is one way of explaining why youth is not innocent. Simply put: you can be born bad. It may be that evil young people are born to bad families or that there is something in their genes. There was a school of thought which suggested that you could detect likely criminals from the shape of their head or from the space between their eyes and you can still hear references to this kind of thinking in today's political speeches on crime.

Stories and myths

Most of the information that is either fed to us or which we feed to each other comes in the form of a story. Stories should have a plot, characters and narrative. So it is in our understanding of life. We will tend to organize our understanding of social events so that they fit around stories. The news media is a powerful reinforcement of this idea. News essentially forces us to ask simple key questions about events – what happened, etc? When we label people we do so in the context of common sense and so when you are constructing key messages about yourself you will need to take account of this way of explaining the world.

Inevitably, life is more complex than the story structure will allow. However, we are able to subjugate some details in favour of others. We will pull out the main characters, the main causes and trends. We are also accustomed to this practice – the news media remind us daily that the complex can be made simple. The multi-layered nature of our lives can be stripped down to the bare bones. And what, in the end, we want to know is what happened, who did it happen to, where and when, how and, most importantly, why?

Here are some examples of organizing concepts which underpin stories used regularly to explain events:

Local boy made good

A simple story in which we are reminded that everyone comes from somewhere. Even the President of America started as an ordinary person. Perhaps we all dream that we will be able to return to our home town (many of us never leave) as the person we always knew we were (but others didn't recognize).

The good Samaritan

A story which reinforces the selflessness of some individuals. The good Samaritan will act in others' interests where there are no incentives for them to do so. Particularly appealing in the context of the me-first nineties, it can be used to reinforce the essential goodness of people.

Mother love

The idea that no matter what a child does, his or her mother will still love and forgive. Promoted through popular stories of wizened mothers visiting their thug-sons in prison. In that sense, it's both a 'factual' and a fictional story.

Blood is thicker than water

Nothing is stronger than family ties. It is popularized via stories of children seeking out their long-lost relatives which can be found in the local and national press. But it is perhaps most famously promoted through programmes such as *Hearts of Gold* where long-lost relatives are reunited in full view of national television audiences. It also helps reinforce the centrality of the traditional family – not least because it is difficult to imagine children from families of a lesbian couple being united in the same way.

Good will triumph over all

Life is reduced to a battle between good and evil and although it will be a struggle, and appear that evil may have the upper hand, in the end good will triumph.

Forty days in the wilderness

At the root of denial for better outcomes. Reinforces the story of Jesus' temptation in the wilderness with Satan. In our culture it promotes an anti-hedonistic stream of thinking, deferred gratification, which, interestingly, often gets tied up into definitions of middle-class thinking.

Money can't buy happiness

This is often used in support of the status quo. It goes: we can't change the distribution of wealth but money can't buy happiness anyway.

Check out your local common senses. One way of emphasizing the importance of common sense is to consciously think what would happen if you, as a manager, started to communicate outside of it. How would you get through the day with your staff operating outside of the everyday taken-for-granted themes of the office? It would be very hard indeed. What we have sought to demonstrate is that communication, if it is to be effective, must be properly planned. It is vital for middle managers that communication strategies, to be

165

effective, must be rooted in what the organization can achieve. To make anything happen the nine possible gaps between a communication strategy and action must be filled. Further, it is vital that it should take account not only of the things we intend to say but also what we intend to do. And, finally, effective communication must take account of the way we think and interpret the world. On this last point the analysis in this chapter is very much underdeveloped, but hopefully, from a manager's point of view, it should begin to pencil in some of the models which help public relations people make sense of the world.

References

Blair, T (1997) *Leading the Way*, Institute of Public Policy Research

Goffman, E (1959) *The Presentation of Self in Everyday Life*, Doubleday, New York and Mayflower, London

Hutton, P (1997) 'Using research to improve quality and size provision', SMi Conference, Measuring Service Quality

Institute of Public Policy Research (1998) Customer satisfaction research – is it time to move on?

Kennedy, JF (1961) A new generation of Americans, in *The Penguin Book of Historic Speeches*, ed B MacArthur, Viking, London

Scott-Peck, M (1990) *The Road Less Travelled*, Arrow Books, London

Thouless, RH (1939) *Straight and Crooked Thinking*, Richard Clay, Suffolk

Tzu, S (1998) *Art of War*, tr by T Cleary, Shambhala, Boston, USA and Shaftesbury, UK

Index